100 Clever, Funny, and Insigh

When Did Caesar Become a Salad and Jeremiah a Bullfrog?

HOWARD
®PUBLISHING CO.

Martin Babb
Illustrated by Ron Wheeler

About the Author

Martin Babb is currently the associate pastor and serves in the education area at Springfield Baptist Church in Tennessee. He also has served as the associate pastor and worked with the youth at Calvary Baptist Church and Pulaski Heights Baptist Church in Little Rock, Arkansas. He has had articles published in many newspapers and magazines. He lives with his wife, Beverly, in Springfield, Tennessee, and they have two children, Meredith and David.

About the Illustrator

Ron Wheeler has been drawing cartoons full-time professionally since 1980. His call before the Lord is to create cartoons to be a communication vehicle for spreading God's truths. Ron and his wife, Cindy, have been married since 1984, and they home school their three children, Audrey (17), Byron (14), and Grace (10). Ron and Cindy both grew up in Nebraska and have lived in Kansas City, Missouri, for over two decades. You can learn more about Ron and how God gave him this calling and see more samples of his work at www.cartoonworks.com.

This book is dedicated to the memory of my parents, Ray and Mary Babb. They were fine Christian examples of what parents ought to be. I miss their encouragement.

◆

I would like to thank the people of Calvary Baptist Church and Pulaski Heights Baptist Church in Little Rock, Arkansas, and Springfield Baptist Church in Springfield, Tennessee. Most of them enjoyed my writing, and some of them even understood. I especially would like to thank my wife, Beverly, and my children, Meredith and David, for their love and support. They also have a wonderful sense of humor. I would thank my three dogs, Molly, Tiny, and Hershey, but they limit their reading to Christian fiction.

Our purpose at Howard Publishing is to:
- Increase *faith* in the hearts of growing Christians
- Inspire *holiness* in the lives of believers
- Instill *hope* in the hearts of struggling people everywhere

Because He's coming again!

When Did Caesar Become a Salad and Jeremiah a Bullfrog? © 2005 by Martin Babb
All rights reserved. Printed in the United States of America
Published by Howard Publishing Co., Inc.
3117 North 7th Street, West Monroe, Louisiana 71291-2227
www.howardpublishing.com

05 06 07 08 09 10 11 12 13 14   10 9 8 7 6 5 4 3 2

Edited by Jennifer Stair
Interior design by Gabe Cardinale
Cover and interior illustration by Ron Wheeler

Library of Congress Cataloging-in-Publication Data
Babb, Martin, 1952–
    When did Caesar become a salad and Jeremiah a bullfrog? : 100 clever, funny,
and insightful lessons for life / Martin Babb.
        p. cm.
    ISBN 1-58229-427-5
    1. Christian life—Humor. 2. Christian life—Baptist authors. I. Title.

BV4517.B33 2005
248.4'02'07—dc22
                                                        2004060913

Scripture quotations not otherwise marked are from the HOLY BIBLE, NEW INTER-
NATIONAL VERSION®. Copyright © 1973, 1978, 1984 by International Bible Society.
Used by permission of Zondervan. All rights reserved. Scripture quotations marked NLT
are taken from the Holy Bible, New Living Translation, copyright © 1996. Used by per-
mission of Tyndale House Publishers, Inc., Wheaton, Illinois 60189. All rights reserved.
Scripture quotations marked KJV are from the Holy Bible, Authorized King James
Version. Public domain. Scripture quotations marked NRSV are from The New Revised
Standard Version Bible, © 1989 by the Division of Christian Education of the National
Council of the Churches of Christ in the USA. Scripture quotations marked NKJV are
taken from The New King James Version®. Copyright © 1982 by Thomas Nelson, Inc.
Used by permission. All rights reserved. Scriptures marked NASB are taken from the
NEW AMERICAN STANDARD BIBLE®, Copyright © 1960, 1962, 1963, 1968, 1971,
1972, 1973, 1975, 1977, 1995 by The Lockman Foundation. Used by permission.

Contents

1. If You Go Berserk in the Kitchen, Are You Speaking in Tongs? (Lessons from Everyday Living)

2. If Love Makes the World Go 'Round, Why Do I Feel So Square? (Lessons on Loving Others)

CONTENTS

3. When the Going Gets Tough, We Usually Go to Wal-Mart (Lessons on Living through Trials)

4. Are Some Churches Just Grazing Land for Golden Calves? (Lessons from the Local Church)

Contents

5. Contrary to Its Popularity,
Crabbiness Is Not a Fruit of the Spirit
(Lessons on Positive Living
from Negative People)

CONTENTS

6. If Home Is on the Range, Then Someone Is on the Hot Seat (Lessons on Family Living)

7. Life Is like a Garage Sale, and I Keep Getting Marked Down (Lessons for the Down-and-Out)

Contents

8. If You Think You've Got Problems, Consider the Person Who Had to Clean the Ark (Lessons on Servanthood)

9. It's Not Christ's Shoes That Are Hard to Fill; It's the Holes in His Hands (Lessons from the Example of Christ)

CONTENTS

10. Spending Time with the Holidazed
(Lessons from Holidays and Holy Days)

Chapter 1:
If You Go Berserk in the Kitchen, Are You Speaking in Tongs?

IT'S HARD TO SWIM IN A SEA OF DEPRESSION, BUT A SENSE OF HUMOR HELPS YOU TREAD WATER

Humor is a funny thing. It's kind of like a taco—everyone enjoys it, but experts disagree on what makes it good. People laugh at different things. I laugh just thinking about words like *bratwurst* and *lizard*. A baby burping always gets a laugh. But if an adult rips one off he is ridiculed, unless he is in college and then he is elected fraternity president. Teenagers, when mixed with parents, closets, telephones, and emotions, become hilariously funny creatures . . . so much so that living with them sometimes borders on hysteria.

Humor, like Baptists and cockroaches, can be found almost anywhere. For example, there is nothing funny about the phrase *Oligocene fossil beds* (a rich archaeological deposit in South Dakota), unless you use it to describe the sleeping arrangements on our church's senior-adult trips. If I told you the story about making an obscene clone fall, some of you would laugh just thinking about the possibilities. Others would just say, "Huh?"

The old cliché "death by a thousand cuts" (about a company gradually going bankrupt) is not funny. But change one letter and it becomes "death by a thousand cats," a phrase littered with potential for humor in a hairy situation. People always want to "clear the air," a phrase that means to remove any confusion about a situation. However, if you use that phrase in the same sentence with the phrase "truckers and tacos," it takes on a whole new meaning.

The dictionary defines *laughter* as explosive sounds of the voice that express mirth or amusement. I like that. It reminds me of going to the circus. Because of Jesus I believe Christianity should be the greatest show on mirth. Some of the saddest-looking people I know are Christians. Their words are more abusing than amusing. They tell people how happy Jesus has made them, but their face apparently never got the memo.

The writer of the book of Ecclesiastes tells us that there is a time to weep and a time to laugh. Some people never change their clocks. Laughter won't cure cancer, it cannot bring back a loved one, and it will not heal a broken relationship. But God gave us laughter to help us deal with sorrow.

In this life, pain may arrive wearing baseball cleats . . . but laughter makes it leave wearing bunny slippers.

An Urgent Need for Yeschatology— the Forgotten Doctrine of First Things

As I get older, the memories of some of the "firsts" in my life are beginning to fade. In fact, the entire decade of the 1970s is pretty much a blur to me. That could be the result of brain damage incurred from overexposure to leisure suits. Those collars were so big that if you wanted to go outside on a windy day in Amarillo, you had to first get clearance from air-traffic control. The first leisure suit I ever spotted (it eventually was removed with a little baking soda) was covering a Baptist preacher—in much the same way a plague covered Egypt.

As a matter of record, 95 percent of all leisure-suit sightings in the '70s were associated with Baptist preachers. Over the years people came to realize just how hideous they were and began telling so many horrible jokes about them that even today when we see one walking down the street, our first inclination is to point and laugh hysterically (at the leisure suit, not the Baptist preacher).

I do remember my first girlfriend. Her name was Mary, and we were both in sixth grade. She was twelve and I was seventeen. In 1964, sixth-grade boys had two time-tested techniques for getting the attention of sixth-grade girls: either pull their hair or impress them with miraculous feats on the monkey bars. The monkeys usually threw me out and sent me back to the playground, where I was king. Well, maybe not the king . . . more like the jester.

When Mary walked by, I would hang upside down on the bar until she noticed me or until my head exploded, whichever came first. I saw Mary at my thirty-year high-school reunion. When I introduced myself, she said, "Oh yeah, you're the weird boy in sixth grade with the exploding head." Over her shoulder I could hear the monkeys at the bar . . . laughing.

According to my theological dictionary, *eschatology* is the doctrine of last things. Hundreds of books have been written about the Second Coming of Christ. Sometimes it is difficult to distinguish between truth and fiction.

But what about first things? What about our worship of God? What about loving our neighbor? If we are to truly worship God, we must be totally focused on Him and nothing else. Through worship we approach the throne of God and are empowered to love people and to live the abundant life Jesus came to give us.

Yeschatology is the doctrine of saying yes to God and yes to living for Him, not for ourselves. Sometimes we can get so focused on trying to figure out the future that we neglect the here and now.

If we never come to grips with the meaning of Jesus's First Coming, how will we ever be prepared for the Second?

IF THE INCREDIBLE EDIBLE ROAD-KILL BILL PASSES, WILL THERE BE A FORK IN THE ROAD?

Our state legislators once considered a bill that would have made road kill legal to eat. Passage of this bill would create a new state motto: "What you hit this morning in Kentucky could be supper in Tennessee." I am convinced the lawmakers approached this as just another pork barrel and did not understand the ramifications of a bill of this maggotnitude. The cost of changing the menus alone would be gastronomical. New items would include single, double, and cripple cheeseburgers with French flies, squishkabobs, and treadmark chicken. Will that be dine-in or carry-off?

Here is a taste of phrases that would take on a whole new meaning: *cold cuts, flea market, tossed salad, scraping your plate, old-fashioned dinner on the ground, shoulder roast, ground beef, eat crow*, and *hot off the grill*. If late for a church dinner, people will simply say, "No problem. We'll just pick up something on the way."

This will pave the way for auto clubs to offer frequent-fryer miles, depending on the number of chickens that do *not* cross the road. Having leftovers will encourage the singing of "On the Road Again." On pickup trucks, gun racks will be replaced with spice racks. McDonald's will have a new slogan: "If your Big Mac attacks—just run over it again."

The preferred automobile of curbside diners everywhere will be Chefrolet, *fire up the grill* will be changed to *start your engines*, and the dinner date of choice will be a romantic dinner by headlight. For liquid refreshment, there will be the occasional unsuspecting dairy cow that wanders across the highway. Got milk? But be careful. If you hit a cow, you could be arrested for leaving the scene of an "oxdent."

When placed in the context of politics, one cannot help but approach the topic of road kill with a skewed sense of humor. But as in most everything, if we keep our minds, hearts, and stomachs open, we can learn a valuable lesson as we travel down the highway of life—at different spiritual speeds and dining on different spiritual food.

Our lives are composed of a series of events that are a direct result of decisions we made when we came to a fork in the road. One road trusts God; the other ignores Him. Our choices affect how we live. What we decide when we reach that fork in the road can make a difference in whether we feast on the riches of God's grace or settle for road kill.

One way or the other . . . dinner is served.

Taking Time for the Refreshing Paws of Life

To be truly fulfilled in this life, and to have humorous stories to share about pet repairs, each person should have the opportunity to own a dog or be owned by a cat. Nothing beats the sweet aroma of puppy breath and fresh puppy puddles on the carpet, or the loving feeling of a sandpaper-like kitten tongue licking your face and cat claws attaching themselves to your nearest sensitive membrane.

I always wanted to have a puppy and a kitten and raise them together to see if they would fight. I had kids instead. Another barrier that has kept me from having dogs and cats at the same time is the fact that my dog of choice is the Chihuahua. Chihuahuas are not very sociable animals. They are basically bullies. If they had been teenagers in the 1950s, each of them would have worn a little white T-shirt with a pack of cigarettes rolled up in the sleeve.

If you want to acquire a cat or dog, you need to be aware of some subtle differences. Puppy utensils include chew toys, a leash, a collar, puppy treats, and a puppy bed. Brand-new house slippers may be substituted for chew toys, and children's toys make an excellent source for puppy treats. Kitten essentials include a litter box (about the size of Nebraska for some cats), a scooper (for internally disturbed cats you can go to the highway department and rent a front-end loader), toys, and a scratching post. Cats are finicky about scratching posts, and only the nearest soft chair, sofa, or human leg will suffice.

There are roughly fifty-five million cats in the United States. The number of dogs is unknown, but judging from the piles on my front lawn, there is at least one very large one in my neighborhood.

When I was a kid, my family had a collie named Beauty. We eventually had to give her to my uncle because he had more room for her to play and exercise. It was a year before my brother and I could visit, and my uncle warned us not to get too close to Beauty because she had become very protective. As we approached the fence, we called her name. She immediately ran to the gate and raised her paw to shake our hands.

I think about Beauty whenever I read the parable of the prodigal son. God is not pleased when we wander away from Him, but He is always there, waiting to welcome us home and shake our hands. If we took time to pause . . . and look in the mirror, we might realize we are the older brother in the parable. Some of us have wandered away and never really left home.

Remember, we can't shake God's hand if ours are busy pointing fingers.

I HAVE NO TITLE BECAUSE I FORGOT WHAT I WAS WRITING ABOUT

Aging is an interesting concept. The idea of turning fifty seems to have captivated the thoughts of others more than it has concerned me. I was born with a fat belly and limited hair, so I figure I really haven't changed all that much. I simply have not been compelled to write about my birthday. However, the deluge of cards, notes, and gifts (many of which were somewhat suspect in their commitment to good taste) has given me a compellsion. (It has given me more than that, but *compellsion* is the most graphic, yet Barney Fife–like, word I can use in a family-friendly book.)

One wayward soul even brought a cake with a Barbie doll inside, wanting out. That was fine until it came time to go to the men's room to wash the icing off of the doll. As I was innocently giving her a good scrub, a burly construction worker entered the men's room. I don't know about you, but the last thing a burly construction worker wants to see when he enters a bathroom is an aging man standing at the sink washing his doll. It was a Kodak moment.

Until I received all of this attention, I wasn't really concerned about turning fifty. Now after experiencing these events and seeing some people who are over fifty, I am more concerned. I have done some studying this week. In reading one article on aging, I discovered I am supposed to expel my toxins. I don't even know what those are, and I certainly don't want to know how I got them. I am also supposed to eat foods rich in antioxidants. Are those foods that are against beef?

Another important health factor at my age is to rid my environment of as many contaminants (not to be confused with contaminflies) as possible. I work in a church office. I'm around contaminants all the time. Contaminants are my life.

Some people my age have had cosmetic surgery. Even fish have been known to do that. Of course they have to consult a plastic sturgeon. The bottom line of aging is that a person is only as old as the number of magnets on his refrigerator.

Satchel Paige was the first black pitcher in the American League back in 1948, for the Cleveland Indians. He made his last pitch at the age of fifty-nine. I like what he said best of all: "How old would you be if you didn't know how old you are?" I may be fifty, but I feel like twenty-five . . . except when I play softball.

It seems to me that a person could spend so much time worrying about aging that he forgets how to live. I have no plans on doing that. As long as I am breathing, I plan on carrying out God's plan for my life.

Aging is inevitable . . . but I choose not to grow old.

LIVING ON EASY STREET, MEMORY LANE, AND GLORY ROAD

Until I attended my thirty-year reunion, I never realized how many friends I didn't have in high school. I had many acquaintances but only a handful of friends. My best friends were in my youth group or in the band. At the reunion I visited with five people from my youth group. Two had become grandmothers at the age of forty-two. They talked about babies and diapers. I talked about Chihuahuas and carpet freshener.

None of my friends from the band came, so I had to toot my own horn. I wasn't the only one. Actually, there was not as much tooting as there was at the ten-year reunion. Twenty years ago most of them were concerned about making a name for themselves. This time the talk centered on the names of their kids and grandkids. One fellow was the proud parent of an eighteen-month-old son. He was also glassy-eyed and heavily sedated. Before every bite at dinner, he would stare off into space and say, "Open up for the choo-choo."

I really enjoyed watching people's reactions upon seeing someone for the first time in years. There were a lot of screaming women, and just like high school, I was not the object of their screams.

One woman suffered an injury right in front of me. She tried to talk to me and broke her ankle getting off her high horse. I was also amazed at how many in my class had become bilingual. When I talked to them, their words said, "Hello, how are you?" but their eyes said, "I don't have a clue who you are."

Several of my former classmates had not changed much. I evidently have changed. I must not have been bald and overweight in high school. I got more strange looks than a sumo wrestler in a health-food store. The highlight of the reunion was taking a group photo. Unfortunately they stood me next to another bald guy right in the middle. We looked like the "one" and "three" pins at the bowling alley.

I guess everyone takes a trip down memory lane now and then. For some it is not a pleasant journey because they carry more baggage than others. For me it was a fun trip, but I don't want to move there. When I was a child, I lived on Easy Street. The older I get, the more I travel down Memory Lane but the happier I am when I return. As an adult I truly believe I am living on Glory Road.

My high-school reunion reminded me that sometimes we get so hung up on the past, we cannot enjoy the present, and we spend too much time and energy worrying about the future. We cannot worry about what was or what might have been.

We really can't go home again, and if we aren't careful, we could spend a lifetime driving through the neighborhood.

BURGERS, FAST FOOD, AND GOD: LIVING ON A WING AND A PRAYER

When the Mongols were busy murdering and pillaging during the Middle Ages, little did they realize the magnitude of inventing steak tartare, ground meat that eventually became what we know as hamburger. The irony is that hundreds of years later, the only people who can understand the language being spoken through the drive-through speaker at a fast-food restaurant are Mongols. We can put people on other planets, but they better not try to order a corn dog.

The conversation usually goes something like this:

Speaker: "Welcome to Burger/Taco/Chicken World. Would you like to mambo?"

Me: "What? I don't dance."

Speaker: "What? I asked if you would like one of our combos."

Me: "Oh. Sorry. No, I'll just have a cheeseburger."

Speaker: "I'm sorry. We don't have cheese burners."

Me: "What? I said cheese*burger!*"

Speaker: "Oh, sorry. Would you like to catch up?"

Me: "I didn't know I was behind."

Speaker: "I'm sorry, sir. We don't have any beehives, only honey barbecue sauce."

Me: "What? You asked me if I wanted to catch up."

Speaker: "No sir. I asked if you wanted ketchup on your cheeseburner."

At this point in the conversation, I am becoming a fan of canned soup. Out of angry determination, I continue.

Me: "Do you have chicken legs?"

Speaker: "I used to, but I've been working out."

Me: "What? Look, read my lips. Give me a chicken dinner."

Speaker: "Have you had a chicken strip?"

Me: "No, I had one that danced funny, but what's that got to do with anything?"

Speaker: "I asked if you had tried our chicken strips."

Me: "Oh, for crying out loud! Give me some cheese dip!"

Speaker: "Sir, it's nacho cheese."

Me: "I know! It's for my wife!"

Speaker: "What?"

I am fully convinced that if Jesus had been forced to place His order through a fast-food drive-through speaker, then the real miracle at the feeding of the five thousand would have been how that many people could be filled by two gloves and a dish.

Too many of us are guilty of approaching prayer with all the fervor and sincerity of ordering French fries. We pause long enough in our chaotic schedules to roll down our spiritual windows and give God our order. We even get angry if the answer is not what we want. He tells us one thing. We do something else. Do we ever really hear what He is saying, much less thank Him or praise Him for who He is?

Prayer, like worship, is not about us. It is always about God. The miracle in prayer is that God loves us so much, He looks beyond our wants and sees our needs.

The next time you drive up to the speaker at a fast-food restaurant, speak clearly and hope for the best. The next time you pray, listen closely to the Speaker . . . He knows what is best.

COMMUNICATION PROBLEM?
SOMETIMES WE JUST NEED TO BITE OUR TONGUES

This will come as no great revelation to anyone, but I have a cell phone. Because I travel quite a bit, I have a package that includes five hundred minutes of free long distance. (The phone cost eight thousand dollars, but the long distance is free.) My package also includes nationwide coverage, which means I can talk to my family from virtually anywhere in the United States . . . unless I am trying to call from inside Robertson County.

When I attempt to make a call inside my own county, I get varied results. None of them are pleasant, and none of them result in my actually talking to anyone. Sometimes I get a beeping sound. This is not a bucolic chirping sound like a bluebird. This sounds more like a chicken hawk swooping down and getting a hernia trying to pick up a St. Bernard—or someone setting off a nuclear-attack alarm through my phone. (Of course, this alarm could only go through if the nuclear

17

attack occurred outside Robertson County.)

I can try to call my wife at the grocery store for some emergency, like reminding her to get Cheez Whiz, and all I get is what seems like hours of silence after I dial. Do I keep waiting, or do I hang up and try again? About the time I have decided to keep waiting, I hear the nuclear-warning shrill. I have learned something important about cell phones. It is quicker, easier, and more satisfying to throw down the phone in a fit of rage than to spend time searching for the little-bitty button that shuts off the nuclear alarm.

Another irritating response I often get on my cell phone is a condescending, computerized voice that says something like this: "The cellular customer you have dialed is not available at this time. Please try your call again later." This is misleading. What has actually happened is that a fly has inadvertently flown into the air space of my wireless company, thrown a fifty-billion-dollar satellite out of whack, and robbed me of a jar of Cheez Whiz.

Alexander Graham Bell thought he was doing a great thing back in 1876 when he invented the telephone. We have telephones now that can do almost anything, except tell a teenager it's time to do homework. Because of improvements in communication since the invention of the telephone, we can now call a big corporation, do our business over the phone, and never talk to a human being . . . if we listen and follow directions.

For communicating with God, each of us has a tongue, eyes, and ears. Unfortunately, we have not developed our ears to their fullest potential. Just like my cell-phone signal is weakest closest to home, it is sometimes like that with prayer.

God can reach us anywhere in the world, but He has the most difficulty getting through when we refuse to listen because we are so caught up in ourselves.

IF THERE IS SUNSHINE IN OUR SOULS,
WHY DO WE RAIN ON SOMEONE'S PARADE?

Except for the "paper versus plastic" firestorm that once engulfed our nation's grocery stores, I have not gotten involved in controversial issues, mainly because they require forming an opinion. I would rather eat liver than form an opinion. The last time I formed an opinion was in 1973, when my all-male college singing group voted on white shirts, plaid pants, and blue bow ties for our spiffy uniform. Since that fashion nightmare, I have found decisions to be much simpler when I flip a coin . . . or a surprised hamster.

But there is a controversial subject on the minds of everyone from Santa Monica, California, to Clinton, Arkansas. It has created a whirlwind of political activity and has put a cloud over our psyche. On this front I come to you in humble humidity and stationaryness. Hide the children and declaw the cats . . . I need to talk to you about the weather.

CHAPTER 1: Lessons from Everyday Living

The most famous weather predictor ever is Punxsutawney Phil, the Pennsylvania groundhog who comes out of a hole on Groundhog Day and may or may not see his shadow. He is not to be confused with Buckatunna Bubba, the Mississippi possum who comes out of a hole and may or may not see the oncoming truck. I used to have a Chihuahua that would shake like a leaf when a thunderstorm was coming, but he usually calmed down when I took him off the weather vane.

On television we no longer have weathermen but meteorologists. A meteorologist is a weatherman who has been repeatedly pelted in the head by a meteor and then sent to a special school. Others forecast the coming winter by observing the bands on the back of the woolly-bear caterpillar. If the dominant band is Glenn Miller or the Boston Pops, it will be a calm or severe winter, respectively. If the dominant band is Jimi Hendrix, then the world as we know it will soon come to an end.

If you don't like the weather in Middle Tennessee, just be patient. It usually changes in a few hours to something totally different. It can be 70 degrees today and snowing tomorrow, and all too often, we let the weather dictate our moods. Unfortunately, the spiritual and emotional conditions around us can change just as quickly as the weather, and we also have a tendency to let those conditions dictate our moods.

There are too many Christians who approach life like the groundhog or the possum. If we see this or we don't see that, we have six more weeks of a bad attitude. When we should be greeting each day with an air of expectancy and sunshine in our souls, all we can muster is a big chill and a dark cloud of anger.

I guess for some, life will always be mostly cloudy . . . instead of partly sunny.

NOT ONLY THE IDES OF MARCH, BUT ALSO BEWARE THE WAXING GIBBOUS

Many of our country's most severe problems—such as road construction, not having a college football play-off system, and presidential debates—can be explained away with the simple phrase, "Well, there must be a full moon tonight." What exactly is a full moon? Is it a moon that just left a church potluck, or does it involve college students in a moving vehicle? Technically, it is when the sun reflects completely off the moon, creating extreme moonshine.

Each month has its own full moon, given a name by Native Americans, who really had too much extra time on their hands. The January moon is the Full Wolf moon. On this day, males in every singles Sunday school class in the Southern Baptist Convention will howl simultaneously. The March moon is the Full Worm moon. This moon will not come out if there is a chance of an early bird. It is also called the Full Sap moon, indicating the time of the month when music ministers get together.

The moon, like a woman turning forty, goes through some interesting phases. According to the *Farmers' Almanac,* there are only a few choice days each month to perform certain tasks—all depending on the phase of the moon . . . or the woman turning forty. For example, in February 2001 there were only four days good for baking. (Depending on your skill, four days may be more than enough.) How many people have you met and wondered if their chicken was completely baked? Well, they probably forgot to check the phase of the moon to see if it was a waxing or waning crescent.

The same goes for jelly. According to the almanac, there are only two days in January good for preparing homemade jelly. If you try it on any other day, you could end up in a jam. Never try anything under a waxing moon, because that is the time when the moon is not fully illuminated by direct sunlight. Believe me, there are enough people now who are not fully illuminated.

I have never really thought about planning my entire life around the different phases of the moon, although my wife turning forty did affect a few decisions. Without faith we all would be living under a waxing moon, because as I understand Hebrews 11:1 (KJV), which says that faith is "the evidence of things not seen," I am not sure anything is ever fully illuminated.

The way I figure it is that God created the universe, and He knows more about everything than anyone else possibly could. I would much rather be in constant communication with the Creator than the created. I can't imagine going through a day without consulting God.

If God were ever asked how often I talked with Him, I would hate for His answer to be "Once in a blue moon."

Chapter 2:

If Love Makes the World Go 'Round, Why Do I Feel So Square?

Lessons on Loving Others

WHEN WAS THE LAST TIME YOU TOAD SOMEONE YOU LOVED THEM?

Did you know that Tennessee has an amphibian-monitoring program? (It is similar to a deacon-monitoring program but with one big difference. Except for a few areas in rural Mississippi, you seldom see fine restaurants with deacon legs on the menu.) The volunteers involved in this program listen to audiotapes of amphibian sounds to familiarize themselves with numerous frog and toad vocalizations, particularly in how they call each other.

Some use AT&T, but most of the amphibians squeeze their lungs with their nostrils and mouths shut. Air flows over their vocal cords, making a shrill or a croak, and their vocal sacs blow up like balloons—a process very similar to angry librarians. One article I read on the subject also included a picture of a woman and her dog. They were sitting in a chair watching for toads, which is what college upperclassmen do during freshman orientation.

Part of the problem in studying amphibians is distinguishing between frogs and toads. Both have tongues that are attached at the front of their mouths and covered with a sticky substance used to catch insects, sort of like attorneys in New Jersey. They absorb water through their skin and do not drink (the frogs, not the attorneys). Like teenagers, they swallow their food whole.

Some species of amphibians, after eating something poisonous, can actually make their stomachs protrude through their mouths and extract the bad food with their right front legs. I saw a football player do that in my college cafeteria. It was not a pretty sight. Contrary to popular belief, frogs cannot cause warts, but they can stir up a nasty case of toad jam. Frogs tend to be moist and slimy, like people at the beach; while toads are dry and warty, like people in West Texas.

It was an interesting study and one that seems to be necessary. The frog population has decreased during the last couple of years, and the cause could be something potentially harmful to humans. Scientists study frogs to find environmental answers. I continue to be amazed as I realize the complicated nature of God's creation and how everything in our world relates to and affects something else. In God's great scheme of things, even frogs and toads matter.

God's amazing handiwork is even more evident with humans because we are created in His image. Each one of us is loved by God. It does not matter whether we are black or white, rich or poor, frog or toad. We all know people who may be down on themselves with little self-worth. Like Terry "the Toad" in *American Graffiti*, they need to hear that God loves them and cares for them—warts and all. They need to know that we love them. They won't know unless we tell them.

The love of God is one story that must not remain untoad.

HEREFORD TODAY, GONE TOMORROW: A MOOVING STORY OF BOVINE INTERVENTION

S eeing my former pastor on a return visit reminded me of an incident during his papacy here several years ago, when the docile cows of Robertson County came to Timberlake. (These were distant relatives of Mark Twain's jumping frog of Calaveras County.) Except in the form of a burger, cows are not supposed to be in Timberlake, unless they are looking for Broadway remakes of *Oh! Cowcutta!* or *Fiddler on the Hoof.*

The pastor discovered the cows early one morning as he was returning from his ritualistic walk across the lake. His keen ears "herd" a commotion in the woods behind his house so horrible and chaotic, it sounded like the line forming at a potluck dinner. Still clad in his monastic robes, he went to investigate and found cows parading out of the woods and heading for the side of his house. (Important cow fact: in the average herd, there is one bull for every thirty cows. In the average church business meeting, there is much more bull.)

Cows love corn, and what better place to find it than a preacher's lawn? Cows also drink thirty gallons of water a day, so maybe they were looking for the ladies' room. Of course the most obvious explanation was that these cows were extremely poor spellers and thought the flashing neon sign in his yard said Pasture.

The wayward cows sauntered around the side of his house, grazed in his front yard for a while, and then moseyed on across the street, through the neighbor's yard, and eventually out of sight.

There is an important truth to be learned from this almost completely truthful and totally ruminating experience. The cows came and went, but except for the sighting by the pastor and an occasional bellow (by the cows, not the pastor), there was no sign they were ever there. With the exception of one or two piles, they left no mark. It makes me wonder if the same thing could be said about Christianity.

As Christians we are to make a difference in people's lives. The song from the 1960s says, "They will know we are Christians by our love," but all too often the only reason people know we exist is the occasional bellowing and the piles of ill will, bad attitudes, and negative words we leave behind.

Like the cows of Timberlake, we are only here for today, gone tomorrow. Because of that we must ask ourselves a question: are we really making a difference, or are we just grazing?

THE VEILED REALITY OF VIRTUAL RELIGION

I t used to be so simple to be a child. I loved being a simple child. I enjoy being a simple adult. People meet me for the first time and say, "You're simple, aren't you?"

I was an official child (ages six through twelve) from 1958–1964 BC—before computers. It was a time when imagination came through the mind, rather than electricity. I had no Nintendo, XBox, PlayStation, MP3, or laptop computer. I did have an electronic football game with two complete teams of figures that I hand-painted the colors of the San Diego Chargers and Green Bay Packers. When I turned on the power, the offensive linemen would just stand there, the wide receivers would run in circles, and the running backs would head for the opposite end zone. It was like watching the Detroit Lions. I played for hours.

In today's world children and adults have access to virtual-reality games. (This is not the virtual reality I experienced in college when a girl told me that talking to me was almost like talking to a real person.) Virtual reality is a simulation that is not the real thing but makes you feel like you are having fun. You can create dialogue on a computer screen and interact with other players online. You are not physically present, but you are carrying on intelligent conversation with others. It is just the opposite of faculty/board/office/church staff meetings (circle the one of your choice), in which you are physically present, but there is no intelligent conversation.

Scientists use virtual reality to help people with their fear of flying, fear of heights, and fear of the Detroit Lions. There is even an experiment with virtual church visitation, substituting a video or DVD for the actual person. I wonder, if Jesus were here today, would He still heal a blind man with mud, or would He tell him where to look on the Internet for a cure? Would He heal a leper by touch, or would He play a video of a healing seminar?

It seems the more advancements we make in technology, the further we get from personal touch. Do we spend more time hovering over our computer keyboard than we do hugging our children? Do our children have electronic gizmos to keep them busy but no idea how to use their imaginations? Do they know how to hug? Do you?

We serve a personal God. He loves us and wants us to share that love with others. Virtual Christians, virtual ministry, and virtual churches are all unacceptable . . . unless we worship a virtual god.

LIFE IS AN INFORMATION SUPERHIGHWAY, BUT I CAN'T SEEM TO FIND THE ON-RAMP

This is difficult to admit, but with the onslaught of electronic knowledge via the Internet, I am amazed at what I didn't know I don't know. The animal kingdom alone is full of stimulating facts that probably no one knows, except for contestants on *Jeopardy!* I'll share with you some of these facts so you can be the center of attention at your next Sunday school class party. Did you know that you can housebreak an armadillo? The expensive part is covering the bottom of his box with asphalt. Alligators can close their ears. It was proven during a recent rap concert in Florida.

Ordinarily it takes a skunk three weeks to manufacture one ounce of odor. He could have done it in three hours if he watched an NBA game. Elephant tusks, when refrigerated long enough, will explode. It is just difficult to get an elephant to sit in a refrigerator longer than ten minutes. All porcupines float. Be careful blowing them up.

Speaking of stimulating facts, how are you on Bible facts? A lot of people seem to enjoy arguing about what the Bible says. I have some questions for you to look up in your spare time. In Gideon's victory, was it the trumpets and pitchers that did the trick, or had the enemy been served meat loaf for supper? Was wandering in the wilderness any worse than driving from Memphis to Little Rock? Was Jonah really swallowed by a whale, or did he just spend three nights in Miami?

Were Beth-Anoth, Beth Arbel, and Beth-Aven Old Testament cities, or were they the forerunners to the Andrews Sisters? If the pigs had been playing baseball when Jesus sent the demons into them and over the cliff, would that have been the first record of an inside-the-pork home run? Was Lazarus really dead, or was he just on the "inactive deacon" list?

Statistics and interesting facts are useless unless we use them correctly. It is the same with the Bible. It is full of interesting facts and wonderful truths, but if we don't use the Bible to find our way to God, what good is it? What good does it do to quote Scripture but not apply it to our lives? We sometimes spend more time worshiping and debating the Bible than we do living out its truths.

If you want to take the Bible for its word, study the questions that follow. Wasn't Jesus color-blind rather than blinded by color? Which do you think God follows more closely: the vote count of the presidential election or the body count of world hunger?

Let's wade through all the facts, statistics, and points of argument and find our way back to the beauty and simplicity of John 3:16. The gospel is the basic message of the Bible . . . and it's the on-ramp to the superhighway of eternity.

Is There a Height Requirement for the Ride of a Lifetime?

U nlike Boy Scouts, who are warned not to mix gasoline with school-cafeteria burritos, I was never told about the potential side effects of mixing my cryogenically preserved body with amusement-park rides. Several years ago I had the dubious misfortune of taking my youth group to Six Flags over Texas. Ordinarily, this would have been a good thing because I love Six Flags.

However, on this particular trip, the day we chose was also Baptist Youth Day for the state of Texas. There are more Baptists in Texas than there are roaches. Texas has more people than some countries and fewer people than Wal-Mart on Friday night, but on this day, there were twenty-five million Baptist teenagers. It looked like an ant farm had exploded, with all the ants wearing religious T-shirts. Every one of them was in line in front of me.

One ride was called the Cliffhanger, advertised as the "world's first total freefall ride." I rode it right after lunch, and it brought a whole new meaning to the phrase *fast food*. When you're on this ride, time is not the only thing that flies when you're having fun. You could literally watch your stomach pass before your eyes.

I am theoretically opposed to any ride that causes even one of my vital organs the least bit of discomfort. I quickly reach a point of subdued hysteria when I see a ride with a description that says, "Made with floorless cars suspended below a steel track, has six inversions—which turn riders upside down—and can reach speeds of 62 miles per hour." It was an interesting description, in a dismemberment sort of way, but I was not created to travel at the speed of fright. On the "can't wait to try that" list, riding on a roller coaster upside down at 62 mph ranks right up there with eating sushi pie while watching *Swan Lake* performed by sumo wrestlers.

Living the Christian life is similar to experiencing an amusement park. Some Christians prefer to ride on a carousel. They pick their spot and stay on the same horse until the music stops. They don't ever get anywhere because a carousel always goes in circles—only the music changes. Other Christians live life on the Cliffhanger, going from one quick-fix spiritual high to the next . . . with no substance in-between.

Although I am not comfortable riding on a roller coaster, it is a fitting description of my Christian pilgrimage. I have my ups and downs, my thrills and spills, and sometimes I must hold on pretty tight. But I try not to become overly concerned because I know the One who controls the coaster. It is the ride of a lifetime, and anyone with the right heart requirement can ride.

It is not the height of man that matters . . . only the depth of God's love.

You Don't Have to Be a Sandwich to Be Miracle-Whipped

My personality leans toward the skewed side of life. When I was young, I played a little too much above-the-neck touch football with my brother's friends, who had sausage for brains. As a result, whenever I see offbeat religious articles in newspapers or magazines, they always catch my eye. Fortunately, they throw it back so I can use it again.

A few years ago, I read about a "laughing revival" that broke out in a church in Toronto. People were rolling in the aisles and laughing hysterically. It was considered a miracle. If I did that this Sunday, *miracle* would not be your first thought. You would think the peanut butter didn't completely cover my cracker.

Another such article concerned an eighteen-inch statue of the Madonna (the Virgin Mary, not the singer) in a small town in Italy. According to the paper, this statue began crying tears of blood for no apparent reason. I can't imagine anything that

34

would cause a statue to cry tears of blood . . . unless it happened to find itself trapped inside my daughter's closet. Townspeople saw this as a genuine miracle (the bloodstained statue, not the bloodcurdling closet). The miracle in my daughter's closet would be if I could *see* her closet.

In 1978 someone claimed to see Christ's image on a tortilla in New Mexico. I have seen many questionable things on a tortilla, but never anything religious. People have visited an auto parts store in Progresso, Texas, to see a floor stain that resembled the Virgin Mary. When I think of miracles, I do not immediately envision tortillas and auto-parts stores. The real miracle would be knowing what Christ and Mary looked like in the first place.

What is it about the miraculous that not only draws people but also whips them into a frenzy usually reserved for sporting events? Have we become so immune to ordinary Christianity that it takes a bleeding Madonna to remind us that God is alive and working in the world today? Are we so miracle-whipped that we fail to see God in the leaves changing in autumn, in the beauty of a sunset, or in the birth of a baby?

There are hundreds of people all around us who, believe it or not, do not need a miracle. What they *do* need is for a group of ordinary Christians to love them, minister to them, and point them to God—the real thing, not a cloud formation. In God we find the greatest miracle of all: He loved us so much He sent His Son to die for us.

We are not miracle-whipped, but we are miraculously loved. The key to consistent Christian living is knowing the difference.

WOMEN MAY BE FROM VENUS,
BUT MEN LEFT A RING AROUND SATURN

Growing up in the 1950s, the foundation of my relationships with girls was based on the assumption that they were weaker and needed to be protected by my manly self. My theory imploded after I saw my first female roller derby on television involving women who had once been poster children for tooth decay. I'm not saying they were rough looking, but they put their makeup on with sandpaper and had names like Bertha and Lars.

Watching them skate around the rink in those shiny uniforms reminded the casual observer of horrible third world experiments with spandex and water buffaloes. They made the East German Olympic women's wrestling team look like ballerinas. That one event shook my foundation of fearless fortitude, shattered my faith in fragile femininity, shaped my future fear of females, and caused me to acquire an afflictive affinity for alluring alliteration.

After years of observing women and men in their natural habitats (hair salons and auto-parts stores, respectively), I have discovered some alarming differences. Inside the head of every woman is a purse that contains all the major cerebral pieces and car keys. A man's head is a virtual vortex of emptiness. This allows for stadium-sized quantities of ego, a remote control, and a brain about the size of a turnip—although the turnip has a better sense of direction.

Men and women share emotions differently. Women actually have emotions. Some have them sewn into their sleeves. A woman will cry over mushy stuff like a baby's first burp and movies like *Titanic*. Men just burp and watch *Dumb and Dumber*. You don't even realize a man has emotions until a thunderstorm knocks out the cable or cancels his tee time.

What do churches do about these differences? We form a committee and immediately assign the nearest woman to be secretary. A better approach would be to celebrate the differences between men and women, both of whom are created in God's image. God formed dust into a man and a rib into a woman. He knew what He was doing. If He had created woman first, she would have removed all the dust and man would have been formed out of leftover animal parts.

Women such as Mary Magdalene, Mary and Martha, and the Samaritan woman at the well aided Jesus in accomplishing His purpose. The Bible does not say, "The Word became flesh and dwelt among the men." Winning our world to Christ will surely take each of us . . . each one different, each one uniquely gifted, each one serving God.

God so loved the *world*, no matter from which planet we may have arrived.

THE ROAD TO LOVING PEOPLE IS MORE EASILY TRAVELED WITH SMALL STEPS

I was only sixteen when Neil Armstrong got on the freeway in Houston, took a wrong turn in Pasadena, went into orbit, and mooned the world. After a few orbits, he landed in Nebraska. He was about to make a famous quote when angry cornhuskers attacked him. He immediately returned to his module and headed for a safer, more civilized environment. This is where the history books pick up the story and he lands on the moon. Then he opens the hatch to speak, and his face swells up and he nearly implodes. He closes the hatch, puts on his pressurized spacesuit, and tries again. "Houston, I don't think we're in Kansas anymore." Then he turns on his microphone and gives the message about small steaks and giant lips for mankind.

Armstrong discovers the moon has a colorless appearance

and just sits there and absorbs the sun, very much like Enron executives. (So far the moon is the only body in space where humans have landed. Several years ago humans accidentally landed in Texas, but they all died off.)

Other objects that have spent time in space—like the person who invented childproof pill bottles—are on display at the Space, Rocket, and Exorbitantly Overpriced Gift Shop Center in Huntsville, Alabama. They have simulating machines that allow people with a less-than-sensational IQ to experience some of the same sensations as the astronauts, such as the IMAX, short for Indigestion Maximum. An IMAX screen resembles the working end of a roll-on deodorant.

I saw a spaceship launched with two giant boosters attached to it. (Once the capsule is in orbit the boosters fall off, hang around in space for a while, then fall to earth, where they immediately rush up to high-school athletes and give them cash to play football in college.) The astronaut then walks into space to shoot some video, which in turn creates in me a sensation of extreme hurling. I hadn't been that queasy since Roseanne Barr sang the national anthem. If that's what space is like, then I don't want to go.

It seems some people out there feel the same way about church. They hear fighting and squabbling in the church. They see Christians in the workplace acting in a manner that does not speak highly of Jesus. Everything they see from people inside the church is a simulation nowhere near the standard Jesus set. If that is what church is like, they don't want to go.

It doesn't take a rocket scientist to understand the basic theme of the Bible: "God loves you." People need to see genuine love, the kind only Jesus gives. That message is so powerful it doesn't need a booster rocket to go into the world. It just needs you and me. Until we share the story, it simply waits on the launching pad.

Sharing the good news of God's love is a small step for some . . . and a giant leap for others.

Red and Yellow, Black and White—
God's Best Rainbow

O ur country has always been open to receiving people from other lands, which is a good thing. Had our immigrant forefathers not been kicked out of other countries, they couldn't have come here and stolen this place from the Indians. As soon as Europe found out there were only Indians in the New World, and no lawyers or preachers, they began flocking to this new paradise. The Puritans landed at Massachusetts Bay and discovered cooking oil. Then, after tiring of roasting chickens over an open fire, they began frying them. Preachers soon followed.

The Dutch landed on Manhattan Island, bought it for twenty-four dollars, and discovered swindling. Lawyers soon followed. The place was named New Amsterdam, and the people were led by a Swede named Peter Stuyvesant. He was actually from Switzerland but fled from there when he grew weary of watching the Swiss just sitting around drinking mocha and poking holes in their cheese. The influx of the Europeans was spreading. Fortunately, the doctors found a cure and gave everyone an influx shot.

Once the spread of influx was stopped, people began arriving in droves. But the droves were flimsy and would crash on the rocks, so the people began using ships again. The Quakers settled in Pennsylvania and invented oats and motor oil. The Germans also settled in Pennsylvania and began raising female weightlifters. In the nineteenth century, there was a great potato famine in Ireland. Dead potatoes were everywhere, so the Irish came to America.

The Protestants, who came here for religious freedom, were intolerant of the Irish Catholics. Prejudice, which had been limited to the Indians, was now rearing its ugly head everywhere. By the end of the century, people were free to hate Italians, who brought really good pizza; Greeks, who came bearing gifts (we were told to beware of them); and the Russians, who brought us female anvil throwers.

People of all nationalities have found a home in our country. We have broadened our capabilities to show prejudice not only to Indians but to all races and all classes of people. We, as Christians, are not immune. If people from a different part of town and wearing a different style of clothing visit our church, how do we respond? What if they sit in our pew?

When Christ came into our world, He loved everyone equally. Some of his best friends were women. He healed lepers and visited with sinners. His church is to be like a rainbow, filled with all kinds of people with all types of hurts and varying levels of needs.

If we do not learn how to love all people—red and yellow, black and white—God just might get the blues.

IF BEAUTY IS IN THE EYE OF THE BEHOLDER, WHY DO PEOPLE TRY SO HARD TO BE THE BEHELD?

Each year *People* magazine bestows upon some fortunate male the honor of Sexiest Man Alive. I personally have a problem with that title. It is demeaning to call a man sexy. I am considering organizing a protest march or calling the ACLU. We men are more than objects to be spread on the cover of some magazine to be ogled by women who have nothing better to do than sit in the recliner and watch *Oprah*.

In 2003 the winner was Johnny Depp, who, I might add, bears a striking resemblance to me. The magazine had winners for sexiest pop star (Pepsi won), Internet mogul (isn't that something on a downhill ski slope?), and country star (Germany won).

Please do not send me angry letters about comparing myself to Johnny Depp. I am not the first to do this. You would not believe the constant verbal barrage I receive in airports—but then I take a breath mint and everything is fine. Of course I am kidding. Since my paraffin wrap and thermal dip, hardly anyone confuses me with Johnny Depp. However, I do get mail for Captain Stubing on the *Love Boat*.

I am considering getting a makeover on one of those daytime talk shows. On shows like these, one poor soul is told by a special loved one that she has a face only a muskrat could love and her hair is so ugly it proves the theory behind why the woolly mammoth became extinct. She is also informed that her picture, including "before" and "after" shots, will be aired on television in front of fifty-five million people and three lonely muskrats. The makeover artists start with her hair but soon give up and encourage her to begin wearing knee socks.

Why do people spend so much money at health spas and fitness facilities in a search to find themselves and yet begin their journey by trying to look like someone else? Ralph Waldo Emerson once said, "Though we travel the world over to find the beautiful, we must carry it with us or we find it not." God loves us just as we are, and that's what makes us beautiful. We are loved.

Want a complete makeover? Begin on the inside and work your way out. No matter what we may look like on the outside, on the inside we have the potential for beauty . . . or the beast. The winner will be the one to which we devote the most time.

Got a minute? Do something beautiful for someone. You won't be on the cover of a magazine, but you just might be mistaken for Jesus.

Chapter 3:

When the Going Gets Tough, We Usually Go to Wal-Mart

Lessons on Living through Trials

Nothing Heals a Wounded Eagle
Like the Warmth of a Scar-Spangled Banner

It was one of those oddly named wars, like the War of the Roses or the Hundred Years War. Obviously tired from naming the French and Indian War, the Revolutionary War, and the Civil War (How can a war be civil?), the Committee for Naming Wars could only come up with the War of 1812.

From the beginning it was an unusual war. The Americans suffered defeat after defeat. It was such a strange war that the most glorious battle for the United States happened at New Orleans, in January 1815, one month after the war had ended.

By September 11, 1814, the outlook for America was bleak. The British had invaded Washington, D.C., burning the Capitol and the White House. The commanding British general set his sights on Baltimore. He knew he could handle the Orioles and the Ravens, but he was unprepared for the eagle. He bombarded Fort McHenry on September 13 and 14. By dawn on September 15, a Baltimore lawyer who was being detained on a British warship out in the harbor noticed that in spite of the bombing, the American flag was still waving. This young lawyer, Francis Scott Key, was moved to write a poem that eventually became our national anthem.

On September 11, 2001, several hours after dawn's early light, another group bombed America. Planes exploded, buildings collapsed, people screamed, hearts sank, terrorists cheered, and God cried. Within hours a flag was flying at each location. Even before the flag went up, it was waving in the hearts of the firefighters, police officers, and other rescue workers who risked their lives to save others. It was waving in the heart of the president as he joined with religious leaders in prayer for unity, hope, faith, and encouragement. One week later, on top of the rubble, the flag still stood.

History repeats itself. The American flag flew at Fort McHenry. It flies at the U.S.S. Arizona Memorial in Pearl Harbor, and it flies at the Oklahoma City National Memorial. It flies in the heart of every American, whatever the race. Our country is too great and our God is too big to be done in by terrorists.

No one who dies on a day of infamy should die in vain. They didn't in 1941, and they won't now. Since September 11, my interpretation of patriotic songs has forever been altered. I have now seen the rockets' red glare and our spacious skies filled with smoke, but I have also seen God's grace shed on us. The flag still waves, and the eagle still flies. God bless America.

THE RAIN MAY CONTINUE TO FALL, BUT GOD STILL BUILDS BOATS

I have always been fascinated by the biblical story of Noah and the ark. *Ark* is short for *Arkansas*, which means "people with bare feet." The root from the original Hebrew actually meant "large, smelly boat." Put the two definitions together and you get "people with bare feet had no business being on the ark."

You may recall from Sunday school (or from reading *Cliffs Notes*) that, early in the Old Testament—around page five—God told Noah to build a large boat with plenty of ventilation. The cell phone connection was horrible, and Noah began building a three-hundred-cubit-by-fifty-cubit goat. Just as Noah was about to ventilate the goat, God made it clear that He was going to flood the earth and that He wanted to save Noah's family and two of every creature on earth. Noah understood and began building the ark.

This was disconcerting to Noah's friends. All they saw was a six-hundred-year-old man building a big boat in the middle of dry land and practicing animal calls. (Historical side note: In those days, before aerobic exercise, disco music, and nose rings, it was nothing for a man to live six hundred years. Today, with the advent of rap music, low-rise jeans, and the Golf Channel, that life span has been shortened to about seventy-eight years.)

Noah spent the first few nights on the ark discovering why carnivores and herbivores do not mix. This is where the phrase "accident waiting to happen" originated. After forty days and forty nights, the rain finally began to subside, and Noah finally took a much-awaited breath of fresh air.

Why do we treat stories like Noah's Ark as great children's stories but overlook the power of God demonstrated within them? In the story of Noah's Ark, we see God's judgment, mercy, love, and faithfulness, all playing out like chess moves in His master plan of providing for His children.

If we truly believe God was at work in Noah's life, why is it so difficult to believe He is still at work today? He didn't clock out at the end of the Old Testament, nor did He retire after the book of Revelation. Among the many things I have learned from the story of Noah's Ark is this: if God can perform all the miracles He did for Noah, then no matter what circumstances may flood my life, I know He can provide a big enough boat to handle them.

WHY WORRY ABOUT ANTS WHEN THERE COULD BE ELEPHANTS COMING OVER THE WALL

L ife used to be so simple when it came to dealing with ants: crush them with a size 11 shoe, make them listen to disco music, or show them your wedding pictures. Another more scientifically acceptable method was to put sand between two pieces of glass and make an ant farm. This, of course, is impossible. You can make an ant raise cattle, but you cannot make him farm.

Ants live in colonies. Once they get thirteen colonies together, they draft a constitution. Then they go to war, raise taxes, and allow the females to vote. Two or three ants gathered together are not much of a threat, but like waiters who sing "Happy Birthday" to you at a restaurant, if you run into a mess of 'em, they can be a real nuisance.

Ants are no longer a simple problem. According to a newspaper article, there are winged fire ants loose in Texas. This is frightening. Why would a decent, God-fearing winged fire ant choose Texas? Texas has enough loose creatures. But it gets more bizarre. These winged fire ants have killed twenty-three thousand *trout.* I have some serious concerns about this situation. First, Texas was made for carp, not trout. Second, my ichthyologic instincts tell me that trout are water-based animals. Why would ants want to go after live trout? Do the trout lure the ants with crackers and cheese? If they do, how do the trout hold the crackers and cheese? Even if the ants are seduced by the temptation, how do they get to the trout? Do they use tiny bass boats and depth finders and pack little cans of Vienna sausage and lie to their wives about where they've been?

When I go to Texas, I have enough trouble dealing with dead armadillos. I don't need winged fire ants. Ants are cagey creatures. They handle food particles much bigger than themselves with relative ease, because they attack one piece at a time . . . and locating the food never seems to be a problem.

Like ants to a picnic, troubles seem to find us wherever we go, and they come at us from all different directions, in various forms—a family problem, failing health of a loved one, a job situation, or even a spiritual struggle. If we let them, these troubles can get the best of us. But there is a way of dealing with them.

As Simon and Garfunkel sang in "Bridge over Troubled Water": "When you're down and out, . . . I will comfort you." David wrote these words in Psalm 34:17: "The righteous cry out, and the LORD hears them; he delivers them from all their troubles."

God never gives us more than we can handle. That's why we never see winged fire elephants.

THE SQUIRREL MAY BE IN THE HOUSE, BUT YOU DON'T HAVE TO LET HIM NEST

I t was Christmas 1996, and we were returning from a trip to Little Rock. It was great to get home, up to and excluding the exact moment we discovered evidence that a varmint, with considerable climbing capabilities, had been loose inside the house while we were gone.

Actually, "we" didn't discover the evidence. I am decoratively impaired and noticed absolutely nothing. However, it did not take long for my wife, Beverly, to find some strategically placed mouse memos on the bedspreads and other household items, such as sofas, pianos, chairs, clothing, and towels, which are important to hygienically advanced females. I inspected the memos and other surprises—chewed miniblinds, scattered jewelry, and dislodged *Rocky and Bullwinkle* tapes—only to conclude this was not the handiwork of an ordinary mouse, unless his first name was Mighty. I suggested it was a squirrel and headed for the comfort and sanctuary of my recliner (my natural habitat) to watch the movie *Apollo 13*.

Several minutes passed, and my solitude was interrupted by my daughter's cry of "Mom, a squirrel!" After I realized Meredith was not referring to David, her brother, I went to investigate. (When I had time to think about it later, I was much disturbed by the fact that in her greatest hour of fear and terror my daughter cried, "*Mom*, a squirrel!" instead of, "*Dad-the-great-protector-of-my-family*, a squirrel!") When I arrived, the squirrel was sitting in the doorway to the living room, minding his own business . . . until the scream.

Never surprise a squirrel. You have not lived until you have stood in the hallway of your own home and witnessed the launching of a startled squirrel. He covered the ground between the doorway and the fireplace in 1.3 seconds. Having just innocently left *Apollo 13*, my response was, "Houston, we have squirrels!"

Until that moment, the closest I had ever come to an animal in the house (with the exception of a particularly questionable tuna casserole) had been a possum in the basement. (This is not to be confused with the awkward-sounding but somewhat tasty pig in a blanket.) While our son, David, armed only with a flashlight, kept up a vigilant watch on squirrel patrol, we found some sticks and plugged the hole. We believe he eventually made his way out of the chimney (the squirrel, not David).

A similar experience happens to Christians. The "squirrels" in our lives hit us when we least expect them. They sneak in, rummage around, and before we realize it, gain control of our lives and lead us away from the priorities of God, family, and friends. It may be a job that is squirreling away our time from our family or a money problem driving us nuts.

We may not know how the squirrel got in, but it doesn't take us long to realize we cannot remove it without God's help. For our own squirrel, we must arm ourselves with prayer, Bible study, and fellowship with God. We won't keep out all the squirrels, but they won't stand a chance of taking up residence.

How Do You Deal with Creeping Iguanas?

I began playing golf at the age of twelve, mistakenly believing it was a noncontact sport. Early in my Gerald Ford–like career, I hit another golfer in the head, which in itself was remarkable because he was standing behind me . . . two fairways over. While golfing I have had close encounters with squirrels, snakes, rabbits, birds (not birdies), wolves, and one very surprised gopher. Other golfers have not been so fortunate.

A man at a Chicago course bent over to pick up his ball and was attacked by a hawk. This was clearly a case of fowl play. Alligators are a unique problem to Florida courses. One ten-foot male alligator in Tampa became so aggressive that wildlife experts had to help it move to another location. Country music stars gathered for a benefit concert to help pay for the move—they called it Gator-aid. A golfer in South Africa was attacked by an elephant, and a boy in Australia was beaten by a kangaroo. The boy shot 80; the kangaroo shot 72.

Recent newspaper accounts have detailed other dangerous encounters between humans and animals, away from the golf course. A 330-pound black bear was photographed in Gatlinburg, Tennessee, going through Dumpsters. Authorities concluded he was looking for the bear necessities. A man in Michigan went after a possum in his kitchen. He tried to shoot the possum but shot the stove's gas line instead. The kitchen was destroyed. The possum survived. It was an impossumble shot.

One family became so exasperated with wild pigs in their garden, they finally opened a theme park. They called it Jurassic Pork. Finally, tree-living iguanas are creeping onto the island of Anguilla. They were apparently blown off of their own island by a hurricane, still in their trees, and drifted two hundred miles to Anguilla, jumping the last few feet from the trees to the island. These, of course, would be the leaping lizards.

We all expect a few problems in life. They are inevitable. It's the events creeping into our lives unexpectedly that seem to really get us down. No one expects a job layoff, a broken relationship, an injured child, or the death of a loved one. We grieve; we deny; we get angry; we try to move on. Unexpected problems cause a natural display of emotions, and working through them is a lengthy process.

In the midst of trying times, we have these comforting words of Jesus: "Let not your heart be troubled; you believe in God, believe also in Me" (John 14:1 NKJV). We need to trust in God as a way of life rather than as a way out of circumstances. We will still grieve, deny, and get angry, but if we walk with God daily, we can work through expected difficulties . . . and be better prepared for the creeping iguanas.

IT's A DOG-EAT-DOG WORLD,
AND CATS ARE WAITING TABLES

I am glad my Chihuahuas cannot read, because they would have seen a *Time* magazine article about the amenities available to today's dog—ranging from day-care centers to pet motels equipped with Barka Loungers. My Chihuahuas, Molly and Tiny, are offered the no-frills, economy plan of food, water, rest-room facilities, and television.

One of today's pet luxuries is a country club where you must first bring in your dog for an interview. My dogs, who are basically field rats on a caffeine high, do poorly in interviews. I'm not saying they bounce off the baseboards (they can't reach the walls), but they could be the poster dogs for Ritalin. All they do during interviews is sniff, growl, bark, and boof (sounds like a law firm). A *boof* is what happens when a small intelligence-delayed dog barks with its mouth closed, mostly just blowing out its jowls (also sounds like a law firm). As Will

Rogers's dog said, "I never met a lawn I didn't like"—and when it comes to lawn decorations, my Chihuahuas can rumble with the big dogs.

Other advances include experimental medical treatments for dog problems. One dog's biting problem was treated with acupuncture—eight needles inserted between his neck and his hips. It cured him from biting, but now he leaks. Several drugs, including herbal medicines, are being tested for dog ailments. Even Prozac has been used to help treat obsessive or destructive behavior, constant barking, tail chasing, and aggression. Well, that's fine for Congress, but will it work on dogs?

Some dogs suffer from separation anxiety, which causes biting and clawing through walls—but then again, so does watching ice dancing on television. Knowing my dogs, they would get uppity after staying at a dog spa for two weeks and begin using police crime-scene tape to mark their territory.

When you get right down to it, most dogs have a pretty good life—mainly because they have someone to take care of them. Dogs don't have anything on us. We have the Great Shepherd, and the nonbelieving world watches to see what, if anything, is different about us because we have been with God. Life is such a treat, and anytime we fail to live it according to the grace God has given us, we ought to be scolded.

Proverbs 17:22 says, "A cheerful heart is good medicine, but a crushed spirit dries up the bones." A dog wags its tail when it is happy, but in Christianity we see much more tail dragging than we do tail wagging. I wonder sometimes if we don't live in a Christian-eat-Christian world, and Satan is waiting tables. If we are, then we, like man's best friend, are guilty of biting the Hand that feeds us.

I NEED A ROCKY MOUNTAIN HIGH BECAUSE I'VE REACHED A BARRY MANILOW

Many of us probably have several events in our past that bring tears to our eyes whenever we are reminded of them. Mine include spending almost the entire decade of the 1980s looking for a Cabbage Patch doll, receiving the bill for my daughter's prom dress, failing to get either of my Chihuahuas to talk like the Taco Bell dog, and being convinced by my son to buy an aquarium.

We all have special movies that bring us to tears just by thinking about them. Some past favorites (depending on your age) might include *Casablanca, Lassie Come Home, Love Story,* and *Ghost.* I am glad one particular movie was never released: *Bambi and Old Yeller Board the* Titanic. My favorite tearjerker movies of all time are *Stripes, Animal House,* and *Blazing Saddles.*

Scientists have discovered that the ability to form tears is one of the many characteristics that separate us from animals. Other differences include humans being able to build up immunity to off-key solo renditions of "The Star Spangled Banner" and the ability of the human male to totally tune out the female while the female tells him about her day.

Scientists also believe tears were first noticed when one of the early descendants of Adam invented fire. (Although Adam was continually on the hot seat, we do not believe he invented fire.) Of course, once people learned how to start a fire with sticks instead of their fingers, the tears went away . . . until wives discovered their husbands would rather burn their fingers than talk to them. Scientists do agree that tears are healthy and we all need an occasional cry. At our house we just listen to old Barry Manilow records.

Did you ever have one of those days when you felt like crying a river of tears? It is OK to cry . . . even for men. God created us as emotional people. No matter how big a river of tears we cry, He always provides a bridge to the other side. Whether we are from *Chicago, Kansas, Boston,* or a *Foreigner* from *Nazareth,* God can revive us during our darkest and coldest nights.

As Christians, we may shed tears as we go through *Dire Straits,* open wrong *Doors,* or battle with *Temptations* on our *Journey.* We are not alone. Because of God, who composed the music of life and sent us the *Bread* of Life, we can sing with the *Byrds* and soar with the *Eagles.* If we are having a *Three Dog Night,* He can send us a *Creedence Clearwater Revival.* No matter how difficult the circumstances, our task is simple . . . believe in the *Son and Cher* His music.

YOU'VE NEVER REALLY KNOWN FEAR
UNTIL YOU'VE TRIED TO HARPOON A MAD CHIHUAHUA

Not long ago, a daytime talk show had a feature on phobias. A very disturbed woman ran screaming from the stage when another woman brought out a Chihuahua puppy. This was a harmless puppy, not mad dog Chihuahuas like mine. My dogs know no fear, except when they go to the doggy doctor. There they lose their swagger. If they get too scared, they lose more than that.

Recently I took my Chihuahuas for their annual shots. It may not be a big deal to your dogs, but to mine those needles are the size of harpoons and the doctor is Captain Ahab. Holding them down is like watching the Crocodile Hunter grab a snake from behind or Martha Stewart approaching a bad salmon croquette. When we get home, Molly and Tiny pout and mope for a week, milking the ordeal for every ounce of sympathy.

My daughter, Meredith, took Tiny for a walk the other day.

CHAPTER 3: Lessons on Living through Trials

Putting a leash on Tiny is like trying to rope an angry mother at a Little League baseball game. Tiny is a three-pound meat loaf gone bad. She fears no other dog. They were walking down the street, minding their own business, with Tiny stopping every thirty seconds to do her business, when the neighbor's poodle, Ginny, came over for a visit. With her fur trimmed to the skin, Ginny looked like a fire hydrant with legs.

Before Meredith could react—Tiny, having a very small brain, lit into Ginny like a soccer mom going after her daughter's coach, stopping only long enough to do more business (Tiny, not the soccer mom). Within a few seconds, Ginny had her mouth around Tiny's throat. The fat dog had sung, and this opera was over. Tiny disagreed. It only made her madder, and she broke away. Very little damage was done to either dog. Meredith, fresh from her shift in the emergency room at the hospital, asked them both to please fill out some forms.

We all have fears. When I was a child, I became frightened during severe thunderstorms at night. The combination of thunder and darkness was more than I could handle. I would run down the hall and climb into bed with my parents. My mother or father would hold me close. That was my haven. I knew they would always be there during a storm.

I am no longer afraid of thunderstorms. I have other fears. I had fears when I sent my children off to first grade. As a parent I guess I will always have fears when it comes to my children. I just do not let fear consume me. Two of the most overlooked words in the New Testament are *fear not*. Jesus can calm any storm and brighten any darkness I may face.

As a child, I was safe in the arms of my parents. As an adult I am still safe in the arms of the Father.

Come, Let Us Spray

L et's play a game called "Huh?" I will give you some clues, and you try to guess what I am talking about, sort of like listening to a college graduation speech.

They can smell human beings from 115 feet away—no, not New York City cabdrivers. They move at 1.5 miles per hour— no, not teenagers cleaning up their room. They love human blood—no, not daytime talk-show hosts. They like to breed in swamps—no, not used-car salesmen.

They have no teeth—no, not a professional hockey team— but they bite live animals. The females have a long mouth for piercing skin—nope, not an opera singer. They are becoming more prevalent pests as humans invade their habitats—nope, not in-laws. Give up? Well, if you said church secretaries, you were really close, but you should be ashamed of yourself. The correct answer is mosquitoes.

CHAPTER 3: Lessons on Living through Trials

Like relatives during the holidays, it takes more than spraying to get rid of these pests (the mosquitoes, not the relatives). One resourceful farmer has invented a contraption similar to a bug zapper. His machine is heated to 100 degrees and releases a chemical that smells like cow's breath. This lures the generally uneducated and slow-thinking mosquito into thinking he is attacking a living, breathing, warm-blooded victim. When he gets too close, he fries and dies. Sometimes he just shakes and bakes.

This confirms something I've always felt. Bad breath kills. Maybe you have a friend who feels compelled to be right in your face when he talks to you, and his breath smells like he just ate a walrus. One man has packaged that breath and is using it to successfully combat mosquitoes. Only in America. Give me liberty or give me breath.

How do you handle the mosquitoes that life sends your way? Oh, I'm not talking about the literal ones with wings, a bite, and a bloodthirsty look. I am referring to the figurative ones. They do not have literal wings or teeth, but once they grab you, they do not want to let go. These "mosquitoes" have names like impatience, stress, anger, discouragement, worry, and a negative attitude.

The good news is that you don't have to wait for a farmer to invent something to take care of these pests. A Carpenter has already done it. He came, He lived, He loved, He died, He arose, and He ascended. But He did not leave us alone. He left us His Spirit, the Comforter. He does not eliminate the mosquitoes, but their bites heal more quickly.

At church we sing, "Holy Spirit, breathe on me . . ." Now, if we could just package that breath, we would be much better prepared to combat the mosquitoes in our lives.

RAISING PEOPLE ABOVE SEE LEVEL
IS A TASK OF *TITANIC* PROPORTIONS

In much the same way that Peter Pan visited Never-Never Land, I traveled to Los Angeles several years ago and spent six months there one week. I never actually saw Captain Hook, but there were times when I saw some real characters.

Having a few extra days, I was able to enjoy some of the local attractions—many of them viewed from the discomfort of my rental car while trying to survive in fifteen lanes of traffic, with an occasional foray outside to peel the air off of my windshield. Even the two-lane streets had six lanes of traffic. I'm not saying traffic was fast, but I saw baby strollers with pit crews.

Los Angeles is known for its Dodgers. These are people who try to walk down the street after dark. On display in Los Angeles is the *Spruce Goose*, Howard Hughes's wooden flying boat made famous by its flight in 1947. It flew for one thousand feet at an altitude of seventy feet. No big deal. I do that after four cups of coffee.

CHAPTER 3: Lessons on Living through Trials

One of the more extremely large historical objects on display in the area was the *Queen Mary* (the boat, not the woman). You may remember that the English sold us the *Queen Mary* in 1967 because she was old, dried up, worn out, and useless. Then they also sold us the large boat. England was looking for somewhere to unload her, and California seemed to be a natural. Their state motto is "Bring us your huddled masses, your grapes, your computer whizzes, and your extremely large boats now—before we slide completely into the ocean."

That was my last experience with large boats until I saw a documentary about the *Titanic*. She rests at thirteen thousand feet below sea level, where there is very little plant and animal life and no light. The *Titanic* is so far down, there is little hope of ever recovering it.

You do not have to go to Los Angeles or see a movie about the *Titanic* to be reminded that there are people all around us who have emotionally or spiritually sunk to the bottom. Because of problems related to marriage, family, or career, they just sit there struggling. They see no way out, no hope, no light, and no chance of recovery. Some of them are so far down they can't even see God.

Unlike the *Titanic*, rising above circumstances is not a manthing; it is a God-thing. It involves the purpose of the church. The church is in the business of helping people improve their vision so they can see light in the depths of darkness and hope in the midst of despair.

People around us may be living below *see* level, but with God's help, they can be raised up. God has a recovery rate that cannot be matched.

Chapter 4:

Are Some Churches Just Grazing Land for Golden Calves?

Lessons from the Local Church

EVER GET THE FEELING THAT THE WHOLE WORLD IS A FORMAL DINNER AND YOU ARE ERNEST T. BASS?

I have been to New York City . . . or to put it in the vernacular of the *Andy Griffith Show,* Gomer has gone to Raleigh. It was the most eye-opening, tension-filled, knuckle-whitening, brain-draining, mind-numbing, ear-piercing experience of my life . . . and that was just the bus ride with the senior adults. Once we got to New York, everything was fine, except for the traffic. Truth really is stranger than fiction. No one in New York City drives a car. They ride a bus or chance one of the jet cabs.

As a child I heard about the bogeyman and how he might get me, and I was scared. As an adult I have now seen New York City cabdrivers, and I am terrified. In the city a red, flashing Don't Walk pedestrian sign does not mean "don't walk." It actually means that if you are standing anywhere near the curb when it changes, and if there is a jet cab within sight, you have exactly five seconds to live. Crossing the street in New York City will soon be an Olympic sport.

The other bizarre part of the trip was observing the people—mostly those on the outside of the bus. I saw one man wearing a long-sleeved gray sweatshirt, gray shorts, black socks, and red plaid tennis shoes. He had four rings in each ear, three in each eyebrow, and four in his lips. He looked like he was standing too close to a tackle box when it exploded.

No one spoke English, and everyone had a cell phone. It was like listening to Alvin the Chipmunk giving instructions to a speed talker on a caffeine high. The second and third most popular languages were honking and hand gesturing. Hands and fingers were arranged in many colorful and not all together uplifting positions. The most popular language was foreign, and every souvenir store in Times Square had five clerks, all of whom had a name that sounded something like Mufasa Muhammed.

An inscription at the base of the Statue of Liberty contains these lines: "Give me your tired, your poor/ Your huddled masses yearning to breathe free/ . . . Send these, the homeless, tempest-tossed to me." These words are a reminder that our country has a place for everyone, including Ernest T. Bass, an occasional character on the *Andy Griffith Show.* Ernest was a little lacking in social skills and had a difficult time finding his place in Mayberry society.

It is like that in the church. People who may not fit in somewhere else are all welcome in the church . . . at least they are supposed to be. There is an understood inscription at every church's door: "Come to Me, all who are weary and heavy-laden, and I will give you rest" (Matthew 11:28 NASB).

"Huddled masses," "homeless," and "tempest-tossed" . . . God's kind of people—Gomer, Ernest T., and me.

THERE IS A REASON THAT THE BLEACHERS ARE THE CHEAP SEATS

To over-the-hill, bald baseball players, slow-pitch softball is the world's greatest sport. It is considered a spectator sport because overweight softball players are really a sight. I miss playing softball. I miss the spill of the game. I miss standing at home plate, listening to the umpire tell me those immortal words: "You're holding the wrong end of the bat!" I miss running through the outfield at the speed of snail birth, tripping on an especially tall blade of grass, and falling flat on my face.

I miss the camaraderie of my church team when I would come back to the dugout after a bad call, and they would support me by yelling at the umpire. I miss coming home after a tough loss, made particularly interesting because of rain, and my loving, understanding wife giving me those blissful words of marital encouragement: "You better not bring those filthy shoes into this house!"

32. There Is a Reason . . .

My most vivid memory is a game where I came to bat in the last inning with the bases loaded (they had been out all night partying), one out (the other two were semiconscious), and we were behind by one run. I could have won the game with a single or tied it with a sacrifice fly. (For you who are baseball illiterate, a "sacrifice fly" is an insect that enters a room first to test it for pesticides.) A chimpanzee or a carp could have done it.

Unfortunately, the chimp had batted in the fourth inning, and the carp had been caught smoking in the dugout. He had ignored the warnings and had to leave with the sturgeon general. The pitch came; I took a mighty swing and hit a monstrous, worm-defying ground ball to the pitcher. The pitcher flipped it to the shortstop covering second base, and the shortstop threw to first for the double play. Game over. Game lost. All we needed was a sacrifice, and I went for the home run.

I see some parallels in the church. The church is like a softball team, and everybody on the team plays an important role. There are a lot of positions in the church that are filled by volunteer players who love to play the game. The key is getting the players into the right position and every player understanding his or her role. We take our turn at bat and deal with whatever comes down the pike because that is our role as a player.

We don't need more innings or additional umpires—Lord knows we have enough of those in our churches. Churches are not built by an occasional home run, but by many players who are willing to sacrifice. We need more people to get off the bench and step up to the plate. You never know how you will do until you take a swing.

As far back as I can remember, a game has never been won from the bleachers.

WHERE THERE IS NO VISION,
THE BLIND LEAD THE BLIND

It is important that we learn valuable lessons from the people who founded our country. If we don't, we are destined to pay twenty-four dollars for Manhattan once again. The first settlers at Jamestown—Ed and Hortense Settler, with their two kids Dixie and Bubba, and their dog Poochahontas—were strong people. They had vision, courage, the memory of a three-month voyage on a ship with no rest stops, and the freedom to decide the shapes of our states.

Most settlers fled England when the British government refused to let them sing choruses in church. The others, like Frank and Prudence Others, fled England searching for religious freedom because they were not allowed to form committees, thus becoming the first religious group in America. (Historic footnote: Native Americans were actually here first but were not considered to be religious because they danced and had no committees.)

33. WHERE THERE IS NO VISION . . .

Another episode full of courage and vision was the pioneer wagon train from Missouri to California, our country's first attempt at carpooling without video games. This is a wonderful page in history (page seventeen), but page sixteen was torn out, and we were left with no official record of two important incidents. Like air traffic today, wagon traffic back then was routed through Atlanta, thus stretching a six-month trek into a three-year nightmare and sending the luggage wagon to Chicago.

Also, the wagon train actually missed California and landed in Detroit. The driver of the lead wagon was a male and would not stop to ask for directions. They crossed many rivers. But they never should have crossed Ahab and Priscilla Rivers, because they got mad and formed the first committee.

Along with courage and strength, our forefathers needed good eyes to find their way through a new land, but they needed vision to even begin the journey. Success came because the pioneers had a common vision and worked together. Without vision they would have stayed where they were. It is the same with churches who are going nowhere. They have no vision for what is outside the four walls and cannot work together because of disagreements over insignificant matters.

Poor eyesight can usually be corrected. Poor vision is another matter. We must get a vision for reaching the people around us, for that is the mission of the church. Using the past as a guide and not as a rut, we must look forward, because when it comes to vision, we do not need the seeing eyes of men as much as we need saying ayes to God.

Vision is nothing but saying "aye" to what God has already seen.

NOTHING GETS A MAN MOVING LIKE BEING BITTEN IN THE SANCTUARY

The first known usage of the word *bite* in Scripture appeared in the Garden when Eve was tempted by a talking snake to take a bite from the forbidden fruit. Except for a few biting serpents, we do not see much of the word until we get to the land of Moab. The people were called Moabites because they enjoyed the bite of the fruit so much they planted apple trees in order to have some moa.

They were a strange because after they took a bite, they would eat their hands, hence the origin of the phrase *bite the hand that feeds you*. Without hands to pick up food, the Moabites soon became extinct, which is just a kinder, gentler way of saying, "there soon were no Moa." Needless to say, traditions from generation to generation were seldom handed down, and the people pretty much took a hands-off approach to everything.

On the other hand, in times of anger, we are admonished by our children not to *bite their heads off*, yet we are encouraged to bite the head off of a crawdad before eating it. Let us never confuse the two. We say someone's *bark is worse than his bite*, which I've never understood, because it seems to imply that when you meet a really crabby person it's OK to let him bite you . . . just don't let him talk. Newlyweds are described as being *bitten by the love bug*. As time goes by, many of them realize it was only a tick.

We sometimes affectionately remember someone's passing as *another one bites the dust*. If you have ever been in West Texas on a windy day, it could also mean you just yawned outside. My favorite contemporary use is *biting sarcasm*, as in the phrase, "Hey, fella! Do I have a sign on my truck that says 'Please drive as close to my tail as possible,' or are you just stupid?"

We once had a burglar in our church *who bit off more than he could chew*. He was cornered when police saw an open window around midnight and sent in a dog to do some research. That doggy in the window was worth every penny. He found his subject and bit him in the sanctuary. Without further ado the surprised intruder was moved to surrender.

I marvel at God's sense of timing. Maybe we were guilty of robbing God of His tithe or stealing time away from Him and spending it elsewhere, but for whatever reason, three days before this incident God used our pastor and his message to grab hold of each one of us and bite us in the sanctuary. He got our attention. Now we need to act on it and get in step with His will.

It may be painful, but we must bite the bullet and move forward.

I'm Crying in the Chapel
Because I've Got Georgia on My Mind
(written December 2000, after the resignation of my pastor)

Just when we thought we were over the sickness caused by the political season, the cold and flu season arrived, along with minor irritants such as the pastor resigning and six weeks of bad Christmas movies. The remedy for sickening political campaigns is to turn off the radio or television. Getting rid of other irritants, like long-distance service telemarketers, is not as easy. However, there are some interesting remedies. There is an old Russian cold remedy that says to wedge a clove of garlic between your teeth and cheek. Colds have been known to vanish within hours. So have old Russians.

The holiday season is fast approaching, and the last thing you want to mess with is unwanted gramps. Take two teaspoons of honey at each meal, and gramps will usually disappear within a week to ten days. If you are still suffering from gramps, cover them with cabbage leaves until they go away. Cabbage leaves are especially effective if gas accompanies gramps.

Although there are a few angry and self-serving Herbs out there, there are many gentle and healing herbs used for medicinal purposes. Alfalfa is rich in vitamins and minerals. One side effect is that it makes your cowlick stand up. Thyme can be used as a medicinal treatment for cough. At one time this was very popular with airline pilots. They wanted to see thyme fly.

Ginkgo biloba is an herb that increases blood flow. In 1513 it discovered the Pacific Ocean. Lobelia is a relaxant that relieves muscle spasms. She was also either one of the Pointer Sisters or Fred Sanford's aunt. The leaves of the gotu kola plant are used to promote the healing of tissue. One side effect is that some good tissue may also fall off. In this case, the plant is referred to as the "un-kola."

I enjoy being in the ministry and serving on this church staff, what's left of it. I did not change my personality when I accepted God's call to the ministry. I felt God could use me in all of my strangeness. As a staff member, it is important to have a pastor who is also a friend. No staff member is ever promised a rose garden in any church, but it helps to have someone to walk with you through the thorns.

Please allow me to grieve a little, to shed a few tears. My friend is moving to Georgia. In time I will feel excited for him, but right now I don't feel so good. I do not believe any of the above remedies would be good for what ails me. There is no remedy for the heartache of saying good-bye to someone who has been a friend, a supporter, and an encourager. From experience I understand the concept of time healing all wounds . . . and in this case, I sure would love to see time fly.

A LETTER FROM CUZZIN MERVIN

This column was first published in April 1987, when I was on the staff at Calvary Baptist Church in Little Rock, Arkansas, and we were about to call a new pastor. It is a fictional letter from my Cuzzin Mervin of Lonesome Toe Baptist Church up in the hills. I believe it is relevant for any church looking for a pastor.

Dear Cuzzin Martin,

How's everthang down in the big city? Thangs is hoppin' round here like crickets on a skillet. I figure the biggest news is that our pulpit committee done went and found us a pasture, but he ain't comin' till this summer. They's sayin' he's off at that there Toad Suck Divinity School back East somewhere's gettin' some more learnin'. Anyways, I ain't seen people this stirred up since Chester Dailey's pig shot hisself with a bow and arrow. At our special meetin' with this here praicher, I seen one fella that ain't been to church in two years. He was all excited and so wuz some others, but the funny thang is that they ain't been back since. That jest don't seem right.

That brings me to what I wanna say. All of our people is excited about the new praicher comin', but some of 'em ain't willin' to do nothin' till he gits here. Now, I ain't got much book learnin', but that don't make sense to me, jest settin' around and waitin'. Shoot, if we wuz to set 'round like that on the farm, we wouldn't get nuthin' done and more'n likely lose our crops. I git the feelin' that some of our folks is more concerned with worshupin' the praicher than they is the Lord. We got some here that ain't never liked any praicher we ever had anyways. Where does it say in the Good Book that we gotta like the praicher afore we kin serve and worshup the Lord?

I know you folks in the city don't got this here partic'lar problem, but us folks in the hills is sometimes guilty of puttin' our praichers up there on the same level with the Good Lord and expect them fellas to do everthang fer us. Now, there ain't but two thangs wrong with that. Number one, no matter what some praichers says there ain't a one of 'em that's good enuff to be put on the same level with the Lord. Number two, if the Lord Hisself cain't get church folks movin', then how in a pig's nose do they expect some skinny little whippersnapper from back East to do it? Even the fanciest farmer cain't git no work out of a dead mule.

Well, anyways, it ain't yer problem, and I done burned yer ears enuff. I'll be a'seein' ya at the next possum fry.

Yer cuzzin,

Mervin

THE MOST DAMAGING FROST
IS NOT ALWAYS OUTDOORS

I know it's cold outside, because when I try to put my Chihuahuas out in the mornings for their committee meeting, they don't budge, especially if there is frost on the deck. Just when I almost have them convinced that their feet will not actually stick to the deck, the morning television weatherman says, "It is 27 degrees outside, but because of the windchill factor, it really feels like 134 below zero." That is all it takes. My Chihuahuas start a pitiful, whiny whimper.

The windchill factor is the true temperature against exposed skin when the wind is at a certain level. For example, at 10 mph you can feel the wind against your face ... and depending on who you are with, you can feel the wind beneath your wings. At 20 mph small branches move, and at 60 mph small animals move.

Windchill can also be a factor inside the home, where marriage is a breeding ground for instant climate changes. The more important the holiday, the more potential there is for a big chill. On Mother's Day, for some unknown reason, the climate turns cold when I ask my wife a simple little question like, "Lamb cakes, are you not going to fix supper?" Ask your wife this one before Valentine's Day: "Sugar bunches, is this one of those holidays where I have to buy flowers?"

I like this one on Thanksgiving: "Honey muffin, why don't you clean up the kitchen while I watch football?" Have you heard this one before? "By the way, sweetie pie, did I tell you my parents are going to spend the holidays with us?" Newlywed husbands can expect instant frost leading to blizzard conditions with this line after his young wife cooks her first meal: "Darling, this doesn't taste anything like my mother's cooking."

Windchill is a problem, especially if you are exposed to it for any length of time. No matter how many layers of clothing you wear, you still feel the cold. Unfortunately, you do not have to be outdoors to experience the effects of a chilling frost. An emotional frost can be just as damaging. All it takes is a cold heart. Some people speak with such cold-hearted words that you can almost see frost forming on their teeth.

If there is any place in the world that should be full of warmth, it is the church. We cannot do anything about the temperature outside the church, but we must be able to control the climate inside. When winter arrives, Jack Frost could be nipping at your nose. Just make sure he stops at the nose and doesn't get any lower.

As Christians it seems we, too, often need to be reminded that our hearts were made to house Jesus Christ . . . not Jack Frost.

AREN'T COMMITTEE MEETINGS ONE OF THE SEVEN DEADLY SINS?

The only two things in life that are inevitable are breathing and serving on a committee. In many churches breathing is a prime qualification when considering someone for a committee. To get a more colorful picture of committees, I have researched some little-known quotes. Will Rogers once said, "God made committees a little lower than the angels, and they've been getting a little lower ever since."

Who could forget the fear in the hearts of the colonists when Paul Revere rode through the countryside with his ominous warning: "The British are forming committees! The British are forming committees!" William Prescott followed that warning with his battle cry at Bunker Hill, "Do not fire until you see the whites of their committees." We saw committees at their best in Mel Brooks's 1974 parody of churches in the Old West, *Blazing Committees,* especially the scene with the audiovisual committee sitting around the campfire.

The best way to really understand committees is to ask a question and answer it with the title of a song. What did everyone say as they left that last building and renovation meeting? *We Gotta Get Out of This Place.* What did Bubba do in youth committee that cleared the room? *The Answer, My Friend, Is Blowin' in the Wind.* What short prayer do you say before each finance meeting? *Help Me Make It through the Night.* Why don't you serve on the nominating committee? *Haven't Got Time for the Pain.*

What if I told you that meetings were going to be exciting from now on? *That'll Be the Day That I Die.* Who usually ends up being chairman of the library committee? *Lucretia MacEvil.* Why don't you want to serve on the kitchen committee? *What Kind of Fool Do You Think I Am?* What did the nursery committee come up with as a theme for their potty-training seminar? *Baby, What a Big Surprise.* What is the new standard uniform for the baptismal committee? *Itsy Bitsy Teeny Weenie Yellow Polka Dot Bikini.*

I could go on and say that the early committee gets the worm, and a committee a day keeps the preacher away, but I think you get the picture. Oliver Wendell Holmes said, "I hate being placed on committees. They are always having meetings at which half are absent and the rest late."

We can keep our tongues planted firmly in our cheeks when we joke about committees, but we could not get along without them. The most important thing to remember is that committees are not a power trip but a road to servanthood. If we keep an open mind, a sense of humor, and faith in a patient God, we will do well.

To paraphrase a familiar verse in Matthew 28, "Lo, I am with you always, even until the end of the committee meeting."

THE SECRET TO CHURCH GROWTH . . .
BELCHING COWS

L ike Columbus searching for a world free from high-salaried professional sports figures, people everywhere have been searching for the secret to church growth. I'll let you in on a little secret: I found it.

The secret to church growth has to do with cows and spectacular signs. My revelation began several years ago on a lonely highway between Dallas and Greenville, Texas. There was a sign that read: "30 Cal. Red Angus Purebred, Show Calves, Hybrids." What a novel idea! Give cows firearms. That would explain the Don't Mess with Texas bumper stickers. Give your cattle some art supplies, and they could certainly draw a crowd.

The cover story in a national magazine mentioned that cows are adding to the problem of global warming by letting out a tremendous amount of methane gas through belching. (This is not to be confused with a similar study on church softball teams.) Belching cows may be a downer for the environment, but they would be an obvious attraction at church, especially on potluck dinner days.

There is something attractive about the spectacular. A few years ago, there was a church in Pennsylvania that had trouble with howlers. At different points during the sermon, three women would stand up and begin howling prayers—and it was not even a sermon on tithing! In Whispering Pines, North Carolina, a group of people meet annually at a Christian nudists retreat. I can only assume the ritual at this service does not include howling.

While mulling over these events, it finally hit me like a ton of too-moist pound cake. The secret to church growth is getting a big-name personality to enter our sanctuary—howling, laughing, and riding naked on the back of a .30-caliber belching cow.

Before I could act on this idea and run it by nine committees, reality set in and I heard the words to a country song— something about how Jesus and Mama always love me, even when the devil takes control. Those lyrics were still ringing in my ear when I was reminded of another song: "Jesus loves me this I know, for the Bible tells me so . . ."

The secret to church growth is not man-made tricks or sensational antics, but in church members telling non–church members that Jesus loves them. It is every Christian building a relationship with a lost person and inviting him or her to worship, fellowship, and Bible study.

It's not sensational, it's not supernatural, it's not complicated, and it's not even a secret. It's been in the Bible all these years.

IN THE JAMES BOND CHURCH
YOU REALLY ONLY LIVE ONCE

When I was a child, I loved to play spy games. I would practice my spiety (spying ability) by hiding in the bushes in front of my house and spying on unsuspecting persons while they walked down our street at night. Looking back, I realize I should have practiced my spiety with a flashlight, ultimately avoiding the uncool and non-spylike position of being sprawled out on a pile of doggy dungaroos.

I even filled out an order form in the back of my comic book and sent off for a spy telescope about the size of a pen. I wanted to be able to see a mile away. When it arrived, I could almost see the end of my front porch.

The first recorded spy episode was the story of the twelve spies sent into Canaan. Ten of the spies got together, formed a committee, and made up a negative report. They sent back a parchment that said Canaan was a great place to visit, but the land was full of gnats. Well, it was not an inerrant parchment. The people thought it said giants, got really scared, and decided to form some more committees.

The most famous spy of all is probably James Bond, known as 007. The most recent Bond movie is about a plot to take over Buckingham Palace by a sadistic cleaning company. It is called *On Her Majesty's Linen Service*. Hopefully it will be better than the previous film about a substandard English professor from Mississippi who wanted to rule the world through bad grammar. It was called *Dr. Knowed*.

James Bond wears the finest clothes, eats in the best restaurants, has a great personality, is the epitome of class and charm, and never has a hair out of place. He is the prototype of the twenty-first-century minister of education. He has a gadget to bail him out of every situation, and he prefers his favorite liquid refreshment shaken, not stirred. Stirred changes the flavor.

Did you know that we practice spiety in the church? Oh, I'm not talking about spying ability but superficial piety, spiety. Much like the Pharisees of Jesus's day, we sometimes practice our spiety by saying all the right Christian words and having all the right "churchy" answers, but we never succeed in showing the outside world we genuinely care about people. We spout on Sunday and pout during the week. We fill a pew on Sunday but cause a "p.u." every day thereafter, thus leading some people to believe the church is full of hypocrites.

People everywhere get together on Sundays for Bible study and worship but return home unchanged and unmoved. It does not matter how many gadgets and gizmos we have in our church-growth arsenal to attract nonbelievers. Until the believers inside the church make a heartfelt commitment to love people as Jesus did and take church outside the four walls, then the church will never be anything more than the James Bond church . . . momentarily shaken, but not really stirred.

Chapter 5:

Contrary to Its Popularity, Crabbiness Is Not a Fruit of the Spirit

Lessons on Positive Living from Negative People

GIVE US OUR DAILY BREAD . . .
BUT COULD YOU THROW IN A POTLUCK DINNER?

t my last meeting of Supermarket Shoppers Anonymous, I received some frightening news. People are buying more and more organic food, which is any food wrapped in edible plastic that contains pedals, keys, or pipes. Actually, there are strict requirements for something to be certified organic, as opposed to the 1960s when it was simply a matter of long hair, beads, and intelligence-devoid phrases like, "Wow, man . . . far out!"

For food to be certified organic, a large percentage of the ingredients must come from an organic farm, a farm that uses no harmful chemicals to kill the pests. This creates prime organic foods rich in proteins such as insect larvae. The consummate organic vegetable farmer chooses environmentally safe fertilizers such as compost, fish meal, limestone, and worm by-products that I refuse to discuss. It gives the phrase *tossed salad* a whole new meaning.

Whatever happened to the good old days when we used standard fertilizers like disco records and shredded political campaign speeches? These wonderful fertilizers would fit perfectly with another phenomenon cutting a swath across unsuspecting palates, TVP (texturized vegetable protein). After watching some of the TVP fester at the grocery store recently, I think it could also stand for texturally vague product.

I live by a culinary axiom stating that the more nutritional value a food contains, the more likely it is to taste like pond scum. I learned this as a baby and began launching strained peas and carrots into earth's orbit. It is most disturbing that my generation of baby boomers seems to be responsible for every taste-impaired fad of the last twenty-five years, including bell-bottoms, paisley shirts, and health food.

Most of us seem to get by with our current eating habits, but we sometimes act as if our spiritual diet is suffering. As babes in Christ we start off with a lite spiritual diet of going to church and reading the Bible. Unfortunately, as we get older we learn to spit out what is really good for us because we just don't want to digest it.

We ask God to give us our daily bread but then live like we really don't believe He will. We ask God for forgiveness but then refuse to forgive someone else. We pray for revival but then never make an effort to say a kind word to someone different from us. At some point in our pilgrimage, our theme song has changed from "More Like the Master" to "I Did It My Way," and we can't feed on God's Word because we are already too full of ourselves.

The Quickest Way to a Man's Heart Is through Your Own Mouth

The surviving food from our holiday onslaught has now made its way out of our home. I watched as a little nuclear caravan formed at our refrigerator and made a quick trip to our neighbor's backyard. After presents, food is the most popular part of the holiday season. For that we can be grateful we live in the United States, where our normal holiday diet consists of turkey, cornbread dressing, mashed potatoes, cheese dip, and a roast-beef sandwich with peanut butter and jelly on it.

For certain African tribespeople who live on the shores of Lake Chad, algae are considered a delicacy. If my daughter lived with them, her closet would be the banquet room. In ancient China, mice were a delicacy. In their nursery rhymes, when the mouse ran up the clock, his time had run out. A favorite bedtime story was "Three Bland Mice."

Obviously, the most popular reason for celebrating the holidays is that it gives us an opportunity to bake bizarre desserts and give them to unsuspecting friends as well-intentioned gifts. Here's a holiday riddle: what is the only dessert that can be used as a baseball bat in the summer and then mailed as a holiday gift at Christmas? Hint: the first one was made in Egypt thousands of years ago and is still in circulation. If you said date bread you were close, but the answer is fruitcake. I've never seen anyone actually eat it, but it does get mailed a lot.

Pies are everyone's favorite, but when they were invented in ancient Greece, they were not filled with fruit but with meat or fish. I can hear Zeus and Apollo as children gathered around the dinner table: "More carp meringue pie, please!" In the seventeenth century, berries began appearing in pies rather than fruits. A popular berry in English pies was the dark blue hurtleberry, as in the statement "The baby was tired of being force fed strained fruit. In one final act of defiance, he hurtled his berries."

For every red-blooded and high-cholesterol American, sweets are an important part of our existence. In my diet, Twinkies are a major food group. Some people feel the same way about chocolate. My taste buds light up and send out party invitations when they see sweets approaching. If something sour comes along, they tremble in fear and end up in deep depression.

With that in mind, why do some people insist on filling their mouths and our ears with sour words? Do people like that spend their spare time sucking on lemons? Proverbs 16:24 says, "Pleasant words are a honeycomb, sweet to the soul and healing to the bones." Kind words build us up . . . and kind words, like sweet-smelling bread, rise up from kind thoughts baked in the heart.

Remember, nothin' says lovin' like somethin' from the spiritual oven.

PLEASE ENTER FROM CLEVELAND
DURING CONSTRUCTION

People who work with animals fascinate me. My favorites are behavioral scientists, zoologists, youth ministers, and professional hockey coaches. These people handle snakes, wolves, poor referees, lions, tigers, and bears (Oh my!) like I would handle pancakes. Although when I was at a twenty-four-hour pancake house/bait shop in college one time at two in the morning studying for exams, I did battle some seriously disturbed pancakes. I watch them (the scientists, not the pancakes) on television nature shows as they study signs to learn about habitats of different animals.

These people's brains have not been visited by oxygen. One man, obviously raised by doorknobs, stuck his head into a rattlesnake hole to see if anyone was home. He recognized the diamondback rattler by the diamond designs on its back, in much the same way tourists in Las Vegas recognize Wayne Newton. The scientist sneaked up behind him and grabbed him behind his head to keep from getting bitten. Then he released Wayne and tried the same procedure on the snake.

These hearty professionals seem to have two things in common: scars and bandages. But they learn the same thing from animal leftovers that I learn while foraging through my son's closet or watching people in truck stops. For example, if you see a small scrap-infested area littered with fruits, berries, grubs, honey, fish, rodents, and lizards, you know immediately you are either in a laundry room where a concerned mother just emptied her six-year-old's pockets, or you have entered the lunch buffet at the football dorm in college.

Actually these signs are often misinterpreted as leftovers from a grizzly bear or a teenager. The two are similar. The difference is the grizzly bear has a more balanced diet, better table manners, and won't ask for the keys to the car. If you are in the forest, be careful how you interpret the signs because you sure don't want to meet a teenager during a feeding frenzy.

On a trip through Oklahoma one summer, I saw a sign on a church that read: "Please enter from Cleveland during construction." I assumed there was a Cleveland Street nearby and they were not referring to the city in Ohio, but it did make me wonder about the misleading signals we sometimes give to people who are searching for meaning in life. Like zoologists studying animals to learn more about them, people look at Christians to learn about Jesus.

If scientists studied people who had just encountered you, would they find people who were spiritually encouraged, or would they find spiritual carcasses and a trail of tears, all that was left of a berating frenzy? Are people better off after having been with you? Do you leave a little bit of Jesus behind you? We may not carry an actual sign, but people learn things about us by the words we leave behind . . . and hopefully, they will not confuse us with an old bear. A grizzly can't kill with its words.

Suffering from Howlitosis:
When the Fruit of the Spirit Turns Sour

There may be a cure for something dentists have dreaded and husbands and wives have fought over every morning for years: postnasal drip. Just kidding! Of course I am referring to a much more serious malady: bad breath, or *halitosis*. It is the only health problem everybody else knows you have before you do. The first sign is when your coworkers begin coming to work wearing oxygen masks.

Other signs are when insects put up a no-fly zone around your mouth, the dog begins sleeping in the next room, your toothpaste turns around and goes back into the tube, and rotting fish look to you as their leader. If you ignore these hints, people will confront you and ask questions like, "Do you literally wait with baited breath?" or, "Did you eat a walrus for lunch?" Finally, when your spouse begins using *take one's breath away* as a daily prayer rather than a phrase of wonder—a probable change should be considered.

What do we do? Go to the source. People are oozing too much ozone. This has created an angry atmospheric pressure that is stirring up some of those pesky sulfuric gases in our mouths. These gases are in severe conflict with broccoli parts left over from not flossing, and the resulting bad breath has caused a crack in the ozone layer. This is bad because it allows bacteria to run free, as opposed to charging them. These bacteria break down proteins and transform them into sulfides. These create odor and bad taste and slip into our system undetected across the state line from Kentucky.

These bad sulfides, like Sodium Lauryl Sulfate (and his brothers Sodium Daryl Sulfate and Sodium Daryl Sulfate), help our breath but give us mouth sores and a sudden urge to move to the swamp, check neighbors for fleas, and dance with dead possums. We must replace these evil sulfides with good sulfates that have no odor or taste (much like the person who invented paisley shirts).

For Christians a bigger problem than halitosis is howlitosis (*chronic negativitis*), a constant spewing forth of words that mystify and mortify rather than purify and edify—like the mournful sound of a howling wolf. Like bad breath, howlitosis is a malady everyone else knows you have before you do—they are just afraid to tell you. They may not reach for an oxygen mask as you approach, but neither do they wait with baited breath for you to speak.

What do we do? Go to the source. We need to replace words that curse, criticize, and control with words that bless, build up, and bring peace. Whenever we fail to treat people as the Prince of Peace did, we make a mockery of the fruit of the Spirit. Halitosis and howlitosis are similar-sounding words with very different meanings. So are peacemakers and piecemakers. Blessed are those who know the difference.

UFOs IN THE CHURCH:
CLOSE ENCOUNTERS OF THE UNKIND

During the 1950s, most of the women who were abducted by aliens had one thing in common: at the time of their abduction, they were wearing white-frame glasses and a poodle skirt. This is directly related to a flying saucer landing near Roswell, New Mexico, in 1947. The three most dangerously comical clothing items ever—the Nehru jacket, the leisure suit, and the silk shirt with a collar the size of a Spanish galleon—were all invented in the days immediately following multiple sightings of UFOs, "Unidentified Flying Objects."

With the onslaught of bell-bottoms and platform shoes, the government officially changed this designation to "Unforgivable Fashion Objects." In fact, since 1947 every recorded sighting of a UFO has coincided with a new fashion statement or an office Christmas party.

45. UFO's in the Church . . .

There are three distinct classifications of UFOs. The first is *alien observation*. This is where a person claims to have seen an alien craft or something that looked like it came from another planet, like a '64 Rambler; or to have observed an alien-like form from a distance, similar to attending a Village People concert.

The second is *alien conversation*. This is reserved for persons who have talked with a being they are convinced was an alien, such as an attorney reading a legal brief or a mortgage loan officer reading the loan agreement. These same people who understand attorneys and mortgage loan officers are employed by fast-food restaurants to talk on the drive-through speakers.

The third classification is *alien immersion*. These people are so immersed in UFOs they claim to have seen Elvis talking on a cell phone to his mortgage loan officer while driving a '64 Rambler through a fast-food restaurant with his attorney in the passenger seat.

In reality I am not as concerned about UFOs in the sky as I am about UFOs in the church, Unidentified Flying Objections. No one knows where they originate, but one is reported every time a Christian gets involved in gossip or negative conversation. Like UFOs in the sky, these always draw a crowd. The conversation goes like this:

First Christian: "Can you believe what so-and-so said?"

Second Christian: "Well, I didn't actually hear it, but I've got a friend who said he talked to someone who overheard someone talking to another person who had heard someone talking about it."

Sound familiar? We must be Christlike, never judgmental or holier-than-thou. We must refrain from gossip. That kind of attitude is foreign to everything the church is about, and we certainly do not want to be immersed in it. It should be the goal of every Christian to reduce the number of Unidentified Flying Objections in the church. Has there been a sighting near you lately?

WASTING AWAY AND KNEE-DEEP IN SEWAGE

There is probably an old proverb that goes something like this: "When sewer backs up into den, best place for husband to be is Memphis." The plausibility of that proverb hit me right between my nostrils a couple of years ago when I returned home from a senior-adult trip to Memphis at 10:45 on a Saturday night. Normally, when I return home that time of night, my wife would just greet me with a sleepy "hello." This time was different.

First of all, she was awake, and she greeted me with a stare that could knock down a caribou. Her teeth were clenched, and she spoke these words with a less-than-angelic voice that could have easily been accompanied by an exorcist: "Ask me about my day!" It was one of those teachable moments in marriage communication where I realized almost immediately if I did not ask Beverly about her day, she would reach into my throat and pull out my tonsils. No husband, unless he is brain-dead, could ignore such a James Dobsonesque plea. I asked. I received.

Sewage backup, like hairstyling, is something I had only read about but never experienced. It started as a groaning and gurgling sound coming from the kitchen sink (the sewage backup, not the hairstyling). Unless they are the subjects of a Stephen King novel, kitchen sinks ought not to groan and gurgle, although our sink once voiced some concern over the disposing of a leftover tuna casserole. Then came the tandem of burping tub and toilet. Unless they are in a fraternity house, tubs and toilets ought not to burp.

The final clue that something was not right was when my son went into the garage and discovered a miniature Niagara Falls coming out of the pipes. He got wasted. My wife then called our next-door neighbor, who, having been through this before and having survived dorm life at a state university, was considered a legend in waste management. He and a plumber soon had everything in order. The mind of man once again triumphed over the weapons of waste.

Unfortunately, it is not so simple when we confront the many "wastes" in our lives. God gives us opportunities to serve Him, and we waste them by doing nothing. We are the salt of the earth, but we waste it by never getting out of the shaker, or in some cases, by using too much. God gives us light, and we waste it by hiding it under a bush. At one time or another, many of us seem to pass through the prodigal-son stage of spiritual immaturity.

But probably the biggest waste is with our words. We criticize rather than encourage. We criticize our child's report card for the one bad mark but say nothing about the good ones. We talk about other people in a negative way, never seeing the positive—or worse, we see the positive but are not willing to admit it. We become much better at speechifying than edifying, and if we do it long enough, it becomes the norm for our words, rather than the exception.

Most of all, it took standing knee-deep in sewage to remind me of the many wasted opportunities I have had to tell my family I love them. To put a different twist on an old saying: "Waste is a terrible thing to mind."

BEEF TIPS AND REST STOPS AND LOOSE LIPS AND GIFT SHOPS— THESE ARE A FEW OF MY FAVORITE THINGS

I recently spent three months with some of our senior adults on a ten-day Fall Foliage trip to New England, except with our bunch a more appropriate term would be Fall *Fooliage*. It was the most beautiful and relaxing trip I have ever been on . . . then my plane landed in Buffalo, and I joined them on the bus. Thus began my descent into the world of riding a bus for three hours without stopping. John Glenn may be a famous astronaut, but we had some folks who, had there been one more long ride between rest stops, would have blasted off and gone into orbit.

I am not saying these mild-mannered, squeaky-clean, kind, and gentle people had violent, Norman Bates–like tendencies, but the Oklahoma Land Rush of 1889 was a Bible school parade compared to thirty-two senior adults getting off the tour bus at a long-overdue rest stop. (I know this for a fact because there were several men on our trip who had survived both events.)

We saw Niagara Falls (sort of like watching a bathtub over-flow) and a portion of Canada, then we traveled across New York, Vermont, New Hampshire, Maine, Massachusetts, and Pennsylvania. On the second day we rested. In-between rest stops and gift shops, we ate. Sometimes we ate at rest stops and in gift shops,. Whenever we approached food, innocent bystanders were trampled (of course I'm kidding . . . they weren't so innocent), and the collective sound of our stomachs growling would embarrass a water buffalo.

With one exception, our dining experiences resembled a shark-feeding frenzy. (Important travelers' culinary advisory: never order beef tips and rice in a restaurant where the cows in the pasture are pointing to the mules . . . and laughing.) Too bad I don't have time to tell you about the 2:00 a.m. come-as-you-are prayer meeting gathered around a New Hampshire lodge smoke alarm.

I wish I could tell you about *The Old Man of the Mountain* and *The Old Man of the Bathroom*, but there are three things preventing me from sharing more details: time, tender ears, and a personal fear of nightmarish flashbacks. However, I do want to highlight one particular item. Along with eating, shopping, and riding, there was another common thread that ran throughout the trip . . . everybody had fun. All one had to do was listen to the laughter.

Maybe that would be healthy advice for each of us. It does not mean we must ignore the pain and anguish all around us, but we do not have to let it overwhelm us and sour our attitudes about life. The same God who gives us a time to weep also gives us a time to laugh.

Listen to the laughter . . . it may not be the best medicine, but it really can be like the sound of music to a hurting world.

WITH APOLOGIES TO WILLIAM GOLDING: YOU, TOO, CAN BE LORD OF THE FLIES

If the United States ever gets into a nuclear war with some third world country, like Alabama, I am convinced of one fact. Ants, flies, and car stereos playing loud rap music will survive. Spring and summer is the time of year when pests like ants, flies, and relatives appear from out of nowhere. The most common kinds of ants around here are pharaoh ants and carpenter ants. Pharaoh ants are distinguishable because of their voices. If you listen to them while they carry off your crackers, one crumb at a time, you can hear them mumbling over and over, "Let my people go!"

Of course the best way to get rid of pharaoh ants is to cover your countertop with pictures of Moses. Carpenter ants are easily recognizable because of their little tool belts around their waists, the pencil behind their ears, and the jeans riding too low in the back. They feed on fungus, prominent in decaying wood and my son's tennis shoes. Some people suggest you combat ants with bait stations, designed to infect the ants with poison. I tried them. They were more like rest stops.

As if there were not enough flies anyway, there is a company in Arizona that raises and sells maggots. This is not some fly-by-night organization. They ship fifty million bugs a week to sixty-five thousand customers in the United States and ten foreign countries. (It is an unproven rumor that sales representatives spend a lot of time hanging out at youth-camp dining halls.)

Several years ago the government of Beijing, China, thought being fly-free would increase their chances of hosting the 2000 Olympics. They launched a campaign to get rid of all the flies in Beijing, passed out hundreds of thousands of fly swatters, and held training courses in how to use them. Their motto was "No, Mrs. Chang, use the other end." Needless to say, their efforts did not fly with the selection committee.

Ants and flies will always be with us, and they come in varying sizes. (I used to live in Texas, where the flies are so big they have landing gear.) Insects are a nuisance, but they are not the biggest problem we will face in life. Jesus told us in John 10:10 that He came for us to have abundant life. We cannot do that and spend most of our time worrying about little things that do not really matter in the big scheme of life.

When I was a child, we went on a picnic one Sunday afternoon. The flies soon found us and I started swatting. After a while my dad looked at me and said, "Son, if you spend all your time swatting flies, you're going to miss the picnic." My prayer for each of us that is we not spend so much time swatting flies in the church that we miss the picnic God has spread before us.

A CHRISTIAN SWIMMING IN A SEA OF NEGATIVITY SHOULD BE LIKE A FISH OUT OF WATER

How we abuse the English language never ceases to amaze and amuse me, especially as I travel around the country observing interesting word usages and strange combinations on signs. I saw one sign that said Show Pigs for Sale. Although I have never seen a show pig, I have seen two pig shows: *Porky and Bess* and *Hamlet*. One sign I had not seen before advertised Limousine Cattle. I guess these are the cows with an extra seat in the rear.

Another sign said Small Arms Sale. As far as I could tell, there was no sale on small legs. One eye-catching business was Bob's Tire. Must have been less stressful to sell one at a time. Wilson, Kansas, called itself "The Czech Capital of Kansas." It was an interesting town. I could see they were huge country music fans, because in each of their voting precincts, there was a place to czech yes or no. I was also able to observe several of the locals bouncing up and down the street. These obviously were the hot czechs.

The strange combinations are the best, and also the most misleading. I drove past the Rusty Moose Bed & Breakfast. When I'm eating or sleeping, I don't want to be anywhere near a rusty moose. One sign advertised Gigantic Flea Market. At what point does a flea become gigantic? I saw a business called Booger Holler Self-Storage. Except at a few football games, most popular books on etiquette agree there is never an occasion when it is proper or acceptable for a booger to holler, much less be stored in one place.

One of my favorites was Living Word Tabernacle . . . Burial Service Tomorrow. Apparently, their living word died. Another was Salmon Ruins. I'm not sure I want to see that. The best was this headline in a newspaper, "Boy Bitten by Shark in Coma." How did they know the shark was in a coma?

Some things do not belong together, like the Little Eagle Shelter located next to an archery range. Of course, that might explain why there are no big eagles. Christians and sin do not belong together. In fact, we sometimes go to great lengths to disassociate ourselves from sin . . . or at least a few selected ones. We like to skip over the sins we commit with our tongue.

Some people call themselves Christians, but a positive word rarely finds its way out of their mouths. All they do is gripe, complain, and blame. It is a strange combination. Instead of floundering and being disoriented, like a fish out of water, some Christians take to complaining like they've been doing it all their lives. Unfortunately, they probably have. Like signs gone awry, too many Christians have hearts that say Living Word Tabernacle and mouths that scream Burial Service Tomorrow.

A CURE FOR THE UNCOMMONLY COLD

You are sneezing, wheezing, hacking, dribbling, gurgling, and the envy of every cat in the neighborhood when you cough. What's the problem? There are four possible explanations. First, you have just received a letter from your least-favorite relatives informing you they are skipping the annual Family Reunion Truck and Pig Pull to spend the holidays with you. They are bringing six kids (none potty-trained), a pregnant cat, and little Billy's cracked ant farm.

Second, it could be you are simply having an implosion from testing your wife's new recipe for carp croquets. A third possible explanation might be that you just watched Jerry Springer's new two-part Christmas special: "What Did Frosty Really Have in His Corncob Pipe?" and "Rudolph Used to Be a Moose." The obvious reason is that you just sat through a sermon on tithing. (Ha! Ha! Just kidding. You stood up part of the time.)

The number one reason is this: unlike the NBA season, the cold and flu season has arrived.

Did you know that colds cost us around ten billion dollars annually? Most of that is to pay for interpreters to interpret statements like "I hab a code in by dose." Translated, it means "Why are there so many unrealistic reality shows on television?" The rest of the money is spent on drugs to combat the side effects from the flu shot you took. One cure is the old wives' tale "Feed a fever and starve a cold." But this only works if you have an old wife, and what husband who enjoys breathing would admit that?

Drink plenty of hot liquids, or just shower with your mouth open. Take zinc lozenges. If you are unfamiliar with zinc, it is one of our more trendy metals and attacks a cold in the same way as drinking a Pepsi and then eating the can. Finally, there is chicken soup (the liquid, not the book), which grandmothers everywhere prescribe as a cure for everything . . . except for bad tithing sermons.

We are all familiar with colds, and as parents we can tell when our child is coming down with one, usually on the day before exams. We recognize the symptoms. But what are the symptoms of a cold heart? It could be a person who never smiles or speaks a kind word. Maybe it is a person who is quick to point out the faults in someone else but refuses to see any fault in himself.

There may not be a cure for the common cold, but there is a cure for the uncommonly cold heart. "Let the words of Christ, in all their richness, live in your hearts and make you wise" (Colossians 3:16 NLT). The words of Christ are wonderfully healing, another of the many remedies we find in God's Word.

A dose of Scripture . . . take two, and call the Great Physician every morning.

Chapter 6:
If Home Is on the Range, Then Someone Is on the Hot Seat

Lessons on Family Living

NOTHING TUGS AT THE HEARTSTRINGS LIKE MUSIC FROM A SILENT PIANO

Something has caused me to have deep thoughts, the likes of which I have not experienced since I gave up trying to mentally rescue the castaways from *Gilligan's Island*. We moved our daughter, Meredith, to college. Like any natural disaster, there were several rescue teams standing by. It could best be described as a cross between relocating a small town and organizing a garage sale blindfolded. In just a few hours, we suffered through mournful sorrow, throat-strangling terror, bansheelike screaming, ear-piercing wailing, and delugelike sweating that would embarrass an overweight logger. Then we got the doorway to her room cleared and began packing for the trip.

"Packing for college" has such an innocent ring to it. Don't be fooled. To parents who have survived the ordeal, it ranks right up there with other evil-lurking-beneath-the-surface phrases from parenthood like "What harm can two hamsters do?" "Can I have my birthday party at Chuck E. Cheese's?" and "What we need is an aquarium!"

When I went away to college, I packed everything into a Ford Pinto, including my golf clubs. I had a coffeepot, a hair dryer, and a black-and-white television with an antenna covered with aluminum foil. It looked like a Mars land rover. My closet was two feet wide by one foot deep. It contained all my clothes. Meredith's room was about the same size, but it contained a small Wal-Mart. I am convinced that somehow, in-between watching her color cable television with VCR and being on the Internet and/or telephone, she found time to study . . . assuming she found her desk.

Meredith and her roommate talked on the phone for weeks just to plan their decorating motif: a jungle theme with tigers, leopards, etc. My roommate and I had no motif. The only time our sheets matched was when we didn't wash them for a month, which gave us a jungle odor motif.

Through the years there were two indicators that let us know if Meredith was in the house. The first was the telephone. We knew she was home if the phone was answered after the first ring. The other was the piano. She could not pass by without sitting down and playing. We would hear the piano and know that everything was right in our little world.

Now that Meredith is gone to college, the phone may ring two or three times before we realize what it is, and unless Beverly is practicing for church, the piano is now silent. But you know what? Everything is still right in our world because Meredith is where she is supposed to be, making music of another kind, with a different audience. When I walk by the piano, I realize why God gave us memory. The piano may be silent, but the echo fills my heart.

IF LIFE WERE A FULL-COURSE DINNER, ADOLESCENCE WOULD FALL BETWEEN BROCCOLI AND THE BURP

I was seventeen, in the spring semester of my first senior year of high school, when I had my first car date. Until that time I had only been allowed to date trucks. At seventeen I didn't know that much about women. (At fifty, I only know what my wife and daughter allow me to think I know.)

All through grade school, I thought girls were only good for transporting cooties. (Now, after two minivans, I realize when they grow up and get married, they also come in handy in transporting children to various activities.) By the time I reached high school, I realized that girls could do more than just cry and point at my hair, so I decided to ask one out. After eighteen failed attempts, I got my first date. She had to get off the forklift to answer the phone, but she said yes.

I took two weeks to make myself pretty. To alleviate my acne problem, I plastered my face with a cream that was impervious to water and could only be removed with steel-enforced sand-paper by a professional wearing lead-lined gloves. It almost worked, but a pimple about the size of a peanut survived. Even this did not discourage me. I had an answer. Being a pious teenager concerned about lost souls, I put a Band-Aid on it and decided to tell her I cut myself shaving.

Night fell—actually, I think it was tripped—and it was time for the big date (the experience, not her size). I had my mom's car, my dad's lecture, and a five-pound bag of breath mints, enough to cover that first critical hour. The *pièce de résistance* was dousing myself with an industrial-strength bottle of English Leather. My face was twitching, my legs were shaking, and my hands were sweating. I knew I was either ready for my first date or my hair tonic was eating through my scalp.

Adolescence is like being on a first date that lasts for six years. It is literally a first date with life, filled with awkwardness, fear, joy, sadness, loneliness, and love—often all in the same day. Like the cream covering his face, what's on the outside is not necessarily indicative of what's on the inside of a teenager.

Do you have a teenager in your home? Remember what it was like to be one. These can be the most rewarding years in parenting. Teenagers have some of the same struggles we did, plus others we didn't, and they desperately need our understanding, patience, encouragement, prayers, and love. They sometimes need our lectures, but they never need our condescending attitudes.

Adolescence, as colorful as it is, cannot be seen with the naked eye—only experienced. There is no need to make a reservation. Just enjoy it when you get there. There is room for everyone to experience once. It's a great place to visit . . . but you wouldn't want to live there.

MOVING CONTENTEDLY FROM THE CHORE LIST TO THE DEAN'S LIST TO THE GROCERY LIST

Americans are fascinated with space travel. In the 1960s many of them were simply spaced out.

I have seen the orbiting capsule on display in Huntsville, Alabama. It is about the size of a recliner with twelve thousand gizmos but no remote control. On the luxury scale, it lies somewhere between a 1971 Chevrolet Vega and the men's bathroom at the Palace in Branson, Missouri, where Showmeyour Hibachi plays the fiddle. It was very cramped and not someplace I would like to sit while orbiting the earth (the capsule, not the bathroom).

Thanks to the Star Wars movies, there have been many changes in space travel the last forty years. In the old days, the capsules would land in the ocean and be retrieved by a navy ship that happened to be spying on the Russians in the neighborhood. Now they land on a runway like a real plane.

I have been through many changes in the last forty years of the space race. When I was growing up, my father traveled and my mother worked for an insurance company. In the summer she would sometimes leave my brother and me a quarter to buy a Twinkie, a coke, and a candy bar. It was a huge treat. It was especially nice because we had completed our chore list, which she had left for us before she went to work.

When I went to college, I was fortunate to find myself on the dean's list twice—once for scholastics and once for an incident involving a Ford Pinto and a muddy football field. After seminary I got married, and twenty-four years later I find myself interpreting a grocery list. At work I have a to-do list in my Day-Timer.

Amidst much change, life goes on. I just change lists. No one has ever accused me of being listless. I have had two children and lost two parents. But in the midst of change, I attempt to approach life like the apostle Paul. I try to be content in whatever state I find myself, although I am not sure Paul ever made it to Texas.

THE NIGHTMARE OF BEING AN ABBOTT AND COSTELLO PARENT IN A FREDDY KRUEGER WORLD

Horror movies and I go together like peanut butter and squash, like heavy metal and elevator music, like trees and West Texas. Put me in front of a horror movie, and I have the intestinal fortitude of cottage cheese. It did not take my wife, Beverly, long to discover that I was fright intolerant. One of the first things we did after we were married, once we finished picking rice and dead armadillos out of our clothes, was to go to a horror movie ... as if the wedding rehearsal was not enough.

This particular movie was called *Alien*. I don't remember the final forty-five minutes because my hands were tying my eyelids together, my coat was covering my face, and I was squirming for all I was worth, trying to tear through the bottom of the theater seat. (This fear-induced routine was something I had mastered through years of renewing my car tags on the last day of the month.) From that tender moment on, Beverly's cutesy, cuddly name for me was "spineless, whiny baby."

Some horror movies sneak up on you because the title is subtle. A few examples are *Children of the Corn*, *Last House on the Left*, and *Silence of the Lambs*. You have no clue these are scary movies. However, with titles like *Psycho*, *The Texas Chainsaw Massacre*, *Nightmare on Elm Street 2: Freddy's Revenge*, *Under the Tuna Casserole*, *Don't Try to Steal My Chihuahua's Biscuit*, *We're Out of Beanie Babies*, and *Church Business Meeting This Wednesday Night*, the horror is obvious. My idea of a good horror movie is *Abbott and Costello Meet Dr. Jekyll and Mr. Hyde*. It's a nice, safe, funny kind of horror.

Unfortunately, our children do not live in an Abbott and Costello world. There are no nice, safe, funny kinds of horrors in adolescence that will go away simply by covering our eyes. We see gangs, drugs, and alcohol, but what about the less obvious horrors of loneliness, self-doubt, and depression? Being a teenager is tough. So is being the parent of a teenager. Neither was designed to be a horror, but either can be.

The greatest horror teenagers face is having parents who do not care. Caring parents use love, patience, understanding, and prayer. Prayer and parenting go together like peanut butter and jelly, like heavy metal and earaches, like wind and West Texas.

No matter what horror comes, it's OK to be scared. And just like at the movie . . . you always have Someone holding your hand.

INVESTING IN CHILDREN:
A RETURN NOT FOUND ON THE DOW JONES

A magazine recently ran a cover story about the cost of raising children to age twenty-one, currently $1,455,581 each—of which half goes to a prom dress. The average cost of clothing to age eighteen is a bit over $22,000. You can knock $21,000 off this total if you refuse to buy basketball shoes. This figure changes for parents of babies, depending on the quality of the diapers.

Things to consider in a good retaining wall–enforced diaper are load-bearing capacity, cartoon logo, degree of industrial-strength odor retention, and how many squishy noises it makes when the child runs through the dining room with a full load while you have guests for dinner. The diapers we used for our children ranged from Ninja Turtles and Care Bears disposable diapers to superpolymer lawn-and-leaf bags. For today's baby, modern technology has brought us the super, surround-sound, sumo diaper, built to withstand the breakup of the Hoover Dam. Healthcare per child averaged just over $20,000, which shrinks to $5.38 if you use castor oil, and it varies with each incoming child. Anytime our firstborn sneezed we researched medical books and took her to the doctor. By the time "Boy" arrived we read the *Farmers' Almanac* and raised leeches. (This study did not consider the diagnosis of opinion-infested grandparents.) Food was $54,000—higher at our house because our kids skipped the pea years (when children discover the fun connection between peas, nostrils, ears, catapults, and parental reactions) and zoomed straight from baby food to pizza. In fact, my son's first word was not "Daddy," but he came close. He said, "Paparoni."

A much more practical and cost-efficient solution is to ease children into a diet of Spam and Cheez Whiz. It also helps them develop the delicate intricacies of gastronomically impaired college students.

You cannot put a price tag on events like changing a baby's first diaper or his first bath—events extremely susceptible to video. Is nothing sacred? Other priceless events include a child's first step, waiting through a twelve-hour dance recital to see your daughter's two-minute dance performance, clapping for your son's first hit at the Little League game, or sharing the tears after his first strikeout.

Those of us who have chosen to travel down the road of parenthood (probably in a minivan) realize we cannot buy those kinds of investments with money, but we do go to our memory banks and withdraw hours of pleasure, fun, sweet remembrances, smiles, and a few tears. Ultimately, when it comes to investing love and time in our children, the market is always open . . . and the source should never run dry.

OFF THE PORCH AND INTO THE WORLD:
A LEAP OF FAITH

I love writing about my years in elementary school for several reasons. Number one is that I had a good time, so I stayed until I was eighteen. Number two is the fact that no one from my school is likely to read this book. For me that means no system of checks and balances. Who will know whether I am writing the truth? And number three is that even if they read this book, they are too old to remember the events. Therefore, you must believe me when I use words like *magnificent, marvelous, effervescent, awe-inspiring,* and *saintlike* to describe how other kids referred to me in grade school. Others simply called me Grandpa.

One of the reasons for my immense popularity at Fair Park Elementary School (besides being the only kid who had a driver's license) was my good fortune to have grandmothers with the unique names of Jessie James and Maria Gonzales. (When

Jessie was married a second time, her last name changed from Babb to James.) My grandmothers came from two completely different worlds, literally. One was born and raised in Arkansas, the other in Mexico—later moving to Colorado. One was Anglo, the other Hispanic. One was Baptist, the other Catholic. One spoke English—Southern style, while the other spoke English with a Spanish flavor. But they had three important things in common: they loved me very much, they had a front porch, and when I would play out there, each grandmother would tell me, "Don't get too far from the porch!"

The front porch provided a great opportunity for me to spend hours by myself, playing and reading, not bothering anyone—at least temporarily. It was also a nice place to pass the day without benefit of a clock, to feel the beauty of a rain shower without getting wet, and to use the power of imagination without the hindrance of electricity. It was a perfect place to read a book. It still is. Simply put, the front porch was a great place to be a child, to use all the senses God gave me, and to experience a small portion of His wonderfully created world. It was communication in its most personal and rewarding form, something I fear has been lost to an entire generation.

Even today, in times of stress (sometimes caused by my computer), I often think back to the days of my childhood, my grandmothers (I had two grandfathers, but their names were Jack and Bill, too plain to impress schoolkids) and two front porches. I hope I never lose that childlike sense of wonder and imagination. No matter how far I may go in my life, I will remember the words of two loving grandmothers . . . and I will never be too far from the porch.

ODE TO A DAUGHTER
UPON HER HIGH-SCHOOL GRADUATION

I twas eighteen years ago when the stork came into our home;
It seems like only yesterday, but my mind does tend to roam.
You arrived with screams and cries that were heard all over town;
After twenty cups of coffee, I finally got calmed down.

We took you home from the hospital in a cute little yellow dress;
Had we not forgotten the diaper, it wouldn't have been such a mess.
You laughed, warbled, and cooed, we even heard you chirping;
And as I recall, Daddy's little girl was especially good at burping.

When you were three years old, the stork brought you a brother;
You loved him so very much back then, you tried to be his mother.
When you helped us with his feeding, you struck a pretty pose;
When you helped us with his diaper, you just turned up your nose.

We provided dancing lessons to broaden your education;
I even attended your recitals, with a lot of hesitation.
The first four hours were worth it, for the chance to see you dance;
You moved like Nureyev, the others like bees were in their pants.

You became a teenager, and I asked one question with gloom:
Why does it look like a garage sale exploded in your room?
We showed it to an interior designer who said it was a hoot;
She said if she had to classify it, the motif would be Early Beirut.

We watched *Young Frankenstein* what seemed like fifty times;
Laughing and saying together all those wonderful lines.
There were some words about life that were truly meant for us:
"Stay close to the candle, the stairway can be treacherous."

Through all of your first eighteen years, we've really had a ball;
Through scrapes, scars, boys, and cars, I would change nothing at all.
Now you've finished high school, I really don't know what to say.
You're going off to college; I'll just look to God and pray.

There will be a void because of your absence; I know it is to be;
I'll miss your laugh and your wisecracks; they say you're just
        like me.
It is difficult to see you leave, and I know that it is best;
But there's still a lump in my throat and a pounding in my chest.

Through the years I've held you close, now my little girl is grown;
I can't be there to hold your hand, but you won't be on your own.
When you finally get to Ouachita, simply listen for the chime;
It will remind you that my love will be with you all the time.

In four more years, we'll do this again, another wonderful day;
If financing college is what I've heard, I will have just begun to pay.

Then one day I'll turn around and you'll be walking down the
    aisle;
I'll look back over the years and say, "It seemed like only
    awhile."

I better say one more thing, or I will never again get the chance;
Even as I think of you now, the tears have begun their dance.
It has taken years to get it back because I thought someone had
    lost it;
But the search for Noah's Ark is over; they found it in your closet.

FROM THE NEST TO THE TREES IS FARTHER THAN IT LOOKS

In much the same way as Patton invaded Sicily, and with almost as much equipment, we took our son, David, to college. When we took Meredith three years ago, she and her roommate planned their motif for weeks. You say "motif" to David, and he'll look at you and respond, "Yeah, but hold the lemon."

That's the major difference between girls and boys. Girls have coordinating decorating motifs, with accessories from Pier 1. Boys have three thousand miles of wires and cords, and decorations that could have come from underneath a fishing dock. When we finished getting David settled, there was enough electronic equipment in his room to power a hair dryer that could dry the biggest, most hideous female hairstyle from the 1960s, or light up Pittsburgh ... assuming one would want Pittsburgh lit up.

How could this happen? It seems like only yesterday I was taking him to the doughnut shop on the way to preschool. Then it was hard enough sending him off to first grade, even though he was twelve at the time. Now he's off to college? This is another reason that parenting should come with warning labels and air bags. My heart was not prepared for the impact. Where did the time go? Didn't I see him pitching Little League baseball last year? What about that learner's permit? Has it really been four years? I know he's only been at college a week, but I miss him. He may only be six hours away, but it seems like eighteen years.

It reminds me of the *Andy Griffith Show* episode where Opie accidentally killed a mama bird and became responsible for raising the babies. He bought a cage and spent the next few weeks nursing them, watching them grow, and listening to them chirp. Eventually it came time for him to let them go into the world . . . where they belonged. Andy convinced him he had done all he could humanly do.

With tears in his eyes, Opie opened the door and the birds flew off to the nearest tree, striking up a chorus that could be heard throughout the neighborhood. He looked down at the empty cage and said, "The cage sure looks awful empty, don't it, Pa?" Andy thought for a moment, looked down at the cage and then up at the trees, and said, "Yeah . . . yeah it does. But don't the trees seem awful full!"

Like Opie and the baby birds, all we as parents can do is love our children, listen to them, nurture them, and watch them grow. We do what we can, with God's help. Eventually the time comes for them to go into the world—where they belong—adding their voices to the music around us, leaving their unique marks in God's wonderful creation. They have to fly away because if all the birds stayed in the nest, nature would have no choir. Go outside. Listen. The nest may be empty, but the trees sure do seem full.

ARTIFICIAL INTELLIGENCE: KNOWING MORE ABOUT COMPUTERS THAN YOUR FAMILIES

I have read some unnerving articles about recent discoveries in the area of robotics. (This comes from the Greek word *robotomy*, which is the surgical removal of one's personality, a requirement for television golf commentators.) Putting me with technology is like mixing the Three Stooges with Shakespeare. I need special light just to match my socks.

But it does disturb me when I read about scientists who are attaching microprocessors to the backs of cockroaches. The only thing I have ever attached to the back of a cockroach is the bottom of my shoe. Scientists in Tokyo have created a "face robot"—a life-size, soft plastic model of a female head with a video camera embedded in the left eye. They are having difficulty receiving consistent readings because it keeps stopping to pluck its eyebrows.

These scientists are evidently fascinated by the concept of

artificial intelligence. Where have these guys been? Don't they know our government has been using artificial intelligence for years? Where do they think income tax forms came from? They are even experimenting using robotics to perform long-distance surgery. A doctor in Cut Off, Louisiana, could sit in surgery and through the combined efforts of telecommunications, video, and robotics, operate on a patient in Belfry, Kentucky . . . without the bats.

I can hear the doctor calling the hospital now: "You have reached the Sisters of Artificial Mercy and Virtual Surgery Hospital. If you need surgery, please press 1 now. If you would like to perform surgery, press 2. If you feel you have reached this number in error and would like to talk to an actual person, Ha! Ha! Ha! Ha! Ha! Ha!"

It's a personal thing with me. If I'm having surgery, I prefer my doctor to at least be within arm's length, in case any important organs fall out.

One thing about the people in Mayberry . . . they had heart. I do not see a lot of that today. I am not against technology. Because of it, we can e-mail missionaries and develop Web sites for outreach and ministry. The problem comes when we let machines take the place of personal relationship. No computer can kiss a child's hurt to make the pain go away or snuggle with him during a storm.

Most of us cannot provide our families with the latest in scientific gadgetry, but we can give them our love and our time. Maybe that is why some people know more about computers than they do their own families. Computers are fast. Relationships take time. We sometimes say today that kids have it all, but when you get down to the heart of the matter . . . I wonder.

MAKING ROOM FOR DADDY

In time I will summon enough courage to enter my teenage daughter's room . . . without an invitation or a lease/purchase option on the bulldozer. To describe it as a garage sale gone mad or a colony of seldom-bathed pack rats exploding would not be adequate. I am never certain how interior designers would categorize the common theme running throughout Meredith's décor. (Other things have been spotted running throughout her décor but have yet to be captured.)

Based on the amount of dirt and moisture (enough to harvest a formidable crop of turnips) and the piles of clothing in the floor (more than enough to clothe a small town), I believe the most accurate classification would be an early swamp motif. However, I must praise her. The soiled clothing and linens are arranged in neat piles marked Mold One, Mold Two, and Mold Three—the last one glowing in the dark and beginning to make breathing noises.

CHAPTER 6: Lessons on Family Living

In one of Meredith's weaker moments, she let me go exploring. In one of my weaker moments, I accepted. I armed myself with a flashlight, a gas mask, and a shovel. I saw things I usually don't see unless I eat some bad tofu. It was better than a safari I took one time under the couch cushions.

Among the items I discovered were all the mates to the socks I thought I had lost in the black hole of our dryer, the Loch Mess monster, the entire colony of Atlantis, more lost episodes of *Bonanza*, a pair of jeans in the process of subdividing, and one leftover hamburger that was way beyond Indiglo.

There was so much nuclear pressure being generated by the amount of huddled masses crammed into her closet that if I ever opened the door, the house would implode. Occasionally, when I catch her in the right mood, she bulldozes enough of her room to let me in for another brief visit . . . and a chance to water the turnips.

I feel pretty good about the whole situation until I realize God must look at us in the same way we look at a messy room. He is supposed to be dwelling inside of us through the Holy Spirit, but our lives are so cluttered, spiritually and physically, we just don't have time or room for Him. Physically, we may need to prioritize our schedule with God being number one. Spiritually, we may need to clean up our room.

That's what confession does. It cleans out our soul so God can come in and relax, have room to walk around, and possibly do a little work. He, too, is probably amazed sometimes at what He finds: characteristics and qualities He hasn't seen in us in months, maybe years. God has a purpose for every Christian, and He seems to do His best work with a committed heart . . . and a cleaned-up room.

Chapter 7:

Life Is like a Garage Sale, and I Keep Getting Marked Down

SALE

CHEAP

Lessons for the Down-and-Out

Don't Try to Reach the Promised Land by Being Almost Persuaded

I am deeply concerned about a recent newspaper article. Evidently an asteroid was flying through the galaxy at 36,000 miles per hour (roughly the speed at which my teenager drives through the neighborhood) and missed the earth by 279,000 miles (the equivalent of driving from Nashville to Memphis). Scientists called this event a dramatic near miss (the asteroid, not the drive from Nashville to Memphis. Scientists call that a black hole).

There is even a more terrifying aspect of these asteroids. Like relatives from Alabama, they arrive without warning and are surrounded by a gas cloud. Out of this scenario arise three very disturbing questions: What is an asteroid? Why do teenagers drive so fast? and Do you have any relatives in Alabama? As a summa cum darling graduate of the Barney

Fife School, let me attempt to answer the first question.

Thousands of years ago, when the earth was dull and void, committees were formed, then two planets tried to maneuver into the same parking spot at the Wal-Mart Supercenter and collided. They exploded into little pieces called *asteroids*, sending them into orbit (the asteroids, not the committees. Committees don't have to collide to go into orbit.). Like men sharing their golf experiences, asteroids are supposed to follow a predictable pattern, but sometimes they get busy talking and take a wrong turn.

This can be as horrifying as an errant golf story. When the asteroids get out of their pattern and go berserk, like women at a shoe sale, the only things that can stop them are large objects, such as the earth, the Russian women's Olympic weightlifting team, or a church constitution and bylaws. It was one of these asteroids, one-third of a mile in width (about the same as laying ten NFL linemen end to end) that was headed for earth, causing a scientific buzz, which is also another name for a haircut on people with an IQ of 140.

Near misses are everywhere. They've been around a long time. I believe it began with Adam and Eve. "Do anything but eat the fruit." Oops. Near miss. Lot's wife did almost everything right, but she looked back and became salt of the earth before it was popular. Near miss. The rich young ruler in Luke's gospel kept all the commandments. Not enough. Near miss. Judas spent a couple of years at Jesus's side. Seemed to be on target. Enter thirty pieces of silver. Exit Judas. Near miss.

Turn the page to the twentieth century. We probably have more than enough cults and religions to go around. Only God knows their hearts, but people who put their faith in these cults all have one thing in common: near miss. Sorry. In eternity with God, there are no points allowed for proximity. A near miss could be the difference between Heaven's Gate and hell's door. We all would do well to remember that John 3:16 does not contain the word *almost*. It's just a simple statement . . . and a can't-miss guarantee.

ONCE THE BOX IS OPENED, THE CRAYONS WILL NEVER BE THE SAME . . . AND NEITHER WILL THE ARTIST

As a child I received a paint-by-number set one Christmas. I sometimes purposefully used the wrong color on a numbered shape and lived in constant fear of being hounded by the paint-by-number police. Living life on the artistic edge became the norm because when given a set of crayons, I would not always color within the lines.

In college I discovered sculpture and stuffed the surviving remnants of a less-than-admirable hot-dog pizza into the mouth of a bronze tiger. In my art class, I studied such great artists and sculptors as Michelangelo, Leonardo, Donatello, and Raphael (most famous for their Renaissance portraits of ninja turtles); Vincent van Gogh (the subject of a really cool Don McLean song on his *American Pie* eight-track); Botticelli (also a form of pasta); and Rodin (best known for his statue *The Thinker*. His classic masterpiece was actually misunderstood and mistitled. Rodin had a lisp and in reality patterned this sculpture after his brother-in-law, Earl, who was a stinker.)

One sculptor who definitely worked outside the lines was Gutzon "Rushmore" Borglum, which also sounds like a curious brand of syrup. Of course you recognize the name of the second-most popular attraction in South Dakota involving stoned faces . . . Mount Borglum. (The most popular attraction involving stoned faces is the annual Harley-Davidson Convention in Sturgis.) Mount Borglum is the little-known carving on the reverse side of Mount Rushmore, of four presidential backsides. It is so named because *Borglum* is the Sioux Indian word for "the Great White Father will visit us in four moons."

The more-publicized Mount Rushmore is the largest work of art on earth, not counting the portrait of the Osmond family. Each face is sixty feet high (of the presidents, not the Osmonds). What was to have been a five-year project took fourteen years to complete, like when procrastinating husbands offer to fix something around the house.

I wonder sometimes what kind of coloring book I would have had if I had only used one color and always stayed between the lines. I wonder sometimes what our world would be like today if Jesus, in His efforts to color His world with love, had only used one color and never ventured outside the lines.

We color outside the lines whenever we find a way to take God's message of love to where it's never been, because people who need the gospel are not always living between the lines. God has given every Christian a unique box of crayons. If we will stop worrying about the size of the box, the color of the crayon, or the consequences of straying beyond the lines, with God's help we can color our world.

THE SHIP OF LIFE—THE ONLY SHIP AFLOAT WHERE THE LIFELINE IS TIED TO THE ANCHOR

Spring is in the air. I know this because flights of pollen are landing at my house hourly. There are little television screens all around my house announcing arrivals and departures. My family is allergic to spring and might as well have signs around their necks that say Kick Me, because that is what spring does every year.

We also know it is spring when sales of shotgun shells are down and sales of pencil erasers are up. Beginning April 15, the only people doing any turkey hunting will be the Internal Revenue Disservice. All of their meals will be served at the tax table. In more ways than one, it is "The Season of the Nose— Blowing and Growing" (blowing because of allergies and growing because of the aforementioned tax deadline).

There is something more important about this date in history. It was on April 15, 1912, that the *Titanic* sank, after grossing $300 million at the box office. She was on her maiden voyage from England to Tulsa. Tulsa was not the original destination, but somewhere off the East Coast, her brakes started failing. The captain reacted quickly and changed course for New York City. He forgot to look out his side-view mirror and hit an iceberg. She sank, not because she hit an iceberg, but because no one eighty-five years later would pay $300 million to see a movie about a ship that completed its voyage.

At that time in history, the *Titanic* was the largest ship in the world, able to handle twenty-two hundred passengers and crew members . . . or three hundred holiday fruitcakes. What was supposed to be invincible was, in reality, quite vulnerable and fifteen hundred people went with it to the ocean floor. The sinking was a freak accident, but many of the fatalities could have been avoided had the ship been equipped with enough lifeboats.

It is the same problem in life. We go sailing along in life, thinking we are also invincible and immune to problems. We are totally unprepared for the icebergs that strike us on the ocean of life, and too many people are going down with the ship when it could be avoided.

A popular game show on television gives a player a chance to win one million dollars. He is given three "lifelines" when he is stumped by a question. There is only one lifeline in life, and that is Jesus. An old hymn has these closing lines: "Throw out the lifeline! Throw out the lifeline! Someone is sinking today." Jesus is throwing out the lifeline. We must choose to accept it or reject it. Our final answer determines whether we sink . . . or swim.

THE GOSPEL,
ALTHOUGH COLORFUL IN ITS SETTING,
IS BEST UNDERSTOOD IN BLACK AND WHITE

According to recent newspaper articles, those pesky research scientists are at it again. A group of them at UCLA have been conducting experiments with flies in an attempt to grow additional eyes (on the flies, not the scientists). The study is so controversial that it was put to a vote. Apparently the eyes have it because the scientists discovered similarities in the genes of fly eyes and human eyes.

I don't want to know that I have something in common with flies, although I can't explain my hunger pains when I see dead animals or the warmth I feel in a greasy restaurant. I don't want eyes growing on my wings or antennae, although my fourth-grade teacher did have eyes in the back of her head.

Another group of scientists has experimented with growing extra ears on mice. If I wanted to see a mouse with an ear attached to its back, I would move next door to Stephen King.

However, extra ears would have helped in the little-known nursery rhyme "Three Deaf Mice."

There is another group of scientists that really sticks in my craw, so much so that I have had to see a specialist on two occasions to have my craw enlarged. These are the people who invented the process for colorizing movies. There is nothing more American than eating popcorn popped in a microwave (made in Taiwan) and watching an old black-and-white Sherlock Holmes movie (about an English detective) on my television (made in Japan).

These pesky scientists decided I was not having fun. Millions of dollars later, advanced technology now provides us with black-and-white movies that look like they were shot in pink and green. Colorizing movies is like painting an order of cheese fries in Leonardo da Vinci's *The Last Supper* or taking the cigars out of the dogs' mouths in *Dogs Playing Poker*. You just don't mess with classics.

Through the years the church has tampered with the original gospel story and tried to modernize it to make it more appealing to the masses. The gospel needs nothing man has to offer in order to enhance the magnitude of its meaning. Churches have tried everything from howling prayers to a laughing revival. In our efforts to modernize the message, we have minimized the Messenger.

Instead of teaching people how to make Jesus Lord of their lives, we have downgraded sin and raised a generation of believers who have made Jesus their pal and best buddy. My biggest fear for the church of the new millennium is that the New Testament Jesus has become more culturally convenient than He is scripturally sound.

"For God so loved the world that he gave his only Son, so that everyone who believes in him will not perish but have eternal life" (John 3:16 NLT). That is the gospel story. It is simple and original. There is no gray area. What the church needs to do is stop trying to improve on the gospel . . . and spend more time sharing it.

IF YOU WANT TO GO WHERE THE FISH ARE, YOU MUST FIRST GET OUT OF THE BAIT SHOP

When I was younger and more prone to eat lunch out of an aluminum can, I was an avid fisherman. If the avids weren't biting, I fished for something else. I religiously practiced the good Samaritan method of fishing by casting my bait on one side of the boat while the fish passed by on the other side.

Most of the action took place in the bait shop, where the owner gave grammar-bashing words of wisdom like "The fisrsh arghnit bahitne tohudya." Then he would spit and say, "The fish ain't bitin' today." Nevertheless, I was determined to allow as many fish as possible the opportunity to exercise their uncanny ability to avoid my lures at all costs.

I went for the largemouth bass, so named because it had a mouth that could swallow a hook, spit it out, and give a Bronx cheer . . . all in one breath. There were other fish, such as the wheel of fortune fish and the jeopardy fish, but they were protected by the game warden.

Despite the heavy dose of frivolity in this article, there is a disturbing trend looming on the horizon among fishermen with asparagus-infused brains. Some of them are jumping into the water, finding catfish with their hands, and wrestling them to the surface. This is called "grappling" or "noodling." I call it "This person has brains on a time-share with a plant."

Grappling or noodling a catfish is not high on my list of inspiring images. One newspaper article had a picture of a recently noodled sixty-three-pound flathead catfish with his mouth clamped firmly around the fist of his apparent noodler. I can hear the conversation in the garage now:

Proud son: "Dad, why is your picture in the paper? Did you win the Nobel Peace prize or write a best-selling novel or rescue someone?"

Exuberant father: "No, Son. I noodled a catfish."

I do not believe it was the image of the catfish grappler that Jesus had in mind when He told a group of fishermen to follow Him and He would make them fishers of men. Putting a fist into someone's mouth, literally or figuratively, is probably not what Jesus intended. The style of the catfish grappler may be flawed, but the motivation is legitimate. In order to catch fish, he will literally go where they are.

In all my years of fishing, I've never had one single fish come to me just because I was sitting in the boat waiting. It takes effort, all kinds of lures, and various methods to catch fish. It is the same with fishing for men. God expects us to fish. The catch is in His hands. The problem is that we spend too much time in the bait shop arguing over the bait . . . and while we argue, the "fish" are getting away.

IF WE LIVE BY SWEET 'N LAW AND NUTRA-SAINTS, WE COULD EASILY BECOME NUMB AND NUMBER

It was one of the most terrifying, shocking, appetite-shrinking newspaper articles I have ever read. The article showcased the food of the future, describing how our taste palates will continue to be expanded with artificial flavoring and foods designed to take the place of real food.

As a longtime fan of eating anything that raises my cholesterol, these advancements in food technology terrify me. For example, I could never eat anything called tofu because it sounds too much like a form of athlete's foot. They are even changing one of my favorite foods: tuna. It now comes in pouches. I don't want tuna in pouches. It needs to be in its natural habitat, a can, where I can drain the oil and excess fish parts.

And what about soy burgers? Unless that soy had four legs and moved in a herd, I don't want a burger made out of it. One of the scientists quoted in the article is a "food-science communicator." I don't have much respect for someone who talks to food, although I have noticed that it is much easier to talk to a turnip than to a teenager. A turnip never rolls its eyes in disgust.

I long for the soft-drink commercial that advertised its product as "the real thing." Churches in recent years have faced a similar conflict with reality. Just look around. We now have imitation churches, synthetic Christians, generic Bibles, superficial worship, and hollow commitment. It could lead to salvation experiences based on artificial flavoring instead of the real fruit of the Spirit.

Instead of being Christ's light, we have created a Christ lite. We have been so intent on being seeker-sensitive in our churches that in many cases we have become Savior-soluble. All we have accomplished is to present a watered-down Christ and a diluted gospel to a world that is dying to experience the real thing. If God's mind can be numbed, I hope the church is never the cause.

CAN'T STAND THE HEAT? IN ETERNITY THE KITCHEN WILL BE THE LEAST OF YOUR WORRIES

I am thankful for the machines that exist today to make life easier, especially in the kitchen, where life sometimes dangles on a precarious but somewhat tasty cliff. With microwave ovens emitting nuclear gas and refrigerators emitting nuclear leftovers, most kitchens are just a bizarre death waiting to happen.

I can read the autopsy report now: "Death occurred instantly by a projectile pork roast as a result of an exploding pressure cooker." Pressure cookers are like bad-acting professional wrestlers. Nothing good can happen when either one of them is full of food and under extreme pressure. There is a rotisserie available that cooks a large chicken in thirty minutes, provided he doesn't move around.

Because of advancing technology, we have some dairy farms

where the cows are milked by computer. Then the computer industry turns around and milks us. Talk at dairy conventions consists of whether your cow is formatted. It not only is not your father's Oldsmobile anymore, it is not your mother's kitchen or your grandfather's cow.

We want everything fast, and we want to do as little of the work as possible. There is a firm in Japan that provides, for a substantial fee, fake guests at weddings, mourners at funerals, and someone to visit your elderly parents. For an extra charge, you can get some of the people for hire to cry real tears on demand, much like your average female driver when she gets stopped for speeding. You can probably even hire someone to taste a casserole you tried to fix in that pressure cooker.

The possibilities are limitless. You might be able to hire someone to "ooh" and "ahh" when a friend shows you pictures of their children. When the pastor invites you over for supper, do you find yourself needing emergency wart removal or some other excuse for not going? Now you can hire someone to go to that horrible dinner. Wedding guests rent for $195–$260 if they have a speaking part. There were a couple of people at my wedding I wish I could have paid *not* to speak.

Most of this company's business is relatively normal, like hiring someone to tend your garden, but all of this convenience comes with a pretty hefty fee. It is not a new concept. The Japanese may be way ahead in their technology, but when it comes to provisions, they must take a backseat to God.

In this new business, every imaginable provision has been covered—except one. They have been unsuccessful in finding someone to die for you. As God might say in today's vernacular, "Been there, done that." He took care of that a long time ago on a hill called Calvary. That is the plan of salvation. God made the provision. Jesus paid the fee. Life, death, and eternity have never been the same.

Hash Browns and the Gospel: Scattered, Splattered, Smothered, and Covered

I t was a traumatic and extremely noise-deafening experience when I moved from being a young married adult
without children to a diaper-laden and French fries-
between-the-seats young married adult with children. Before I
had children, I ate in restaurants that actually had cloth napkins
and breakable dishes, and where *Styrofoam* was a foreign word.
These restaurants contained no playground, and the waiters
didn't hover over our table like a crazed minstrel group to sing
"Happy Birthday" in a manner that would make tap-dancing
sumo wrestlers seem wonderfully artistic.

Eating out with young children required driving under a
golden arch or fighting our way past a man in a mouse suit to
enter a circus-gone-mad arena and eat pizza with all the flavor
and texture of a manhole cover. Those were the days.

I mention food because the seven stages in a person's life

coincide with the seven major food groups. Babies like baby food—various-colored runny foods that temporarily fit on a little spoon and will enter the baby's mouth only when the feeding parent makes absurd and embarrassing boat, plane, or train noises. Many parents make other embarrassing noises, but those don't help the feeding situation.

Preschoolers prefer lightweight food. This is any food that can be easily thrown, pitched, or crammed. Older children like finger foods. These are food items that can be held with fingers, strategically placed underneath the table when parents are not looking, and given to a smiling dog. The dog quits smiling when the child tries to slip him pickled okra.

Young teenagers eat medieval food—food that can be catapulted during a food fight. Older teens prefer food that can be consumed in mass quantities, such as pizza and cheese dip. College students enjoy cheap, greasy food that can be paid for by parents and eaten after midnight. Adults eat cafeteria food. This is food on display under a dirty, plastic sneeze guard.

There is a popular eatery that offers hash browns cooked six different ways: scattered, smothered, covered, chunked, diced, and topped. But no matter how you order them, they are still hash browns. The church has done the same thing with the gospel story. The good news of Jesus has not changed in two thousand years, but how we serve it has. We have found new ways to meet people at their greatest need. Sounds sort of biblical, doesn't it?

After all, isn't that what Jesus did? He *chunked* common religious customs of the day to spend time with sinners. Instead of coming to destroy the law, He *topped* it. Self-righteous

Pharisees could not trap Him—He verbally *diced* them into little pieces. Ultimately, Jesus's blood *covered* our sins. Like hash browns, the gospel is not fully understood until it is shared— one way or the other. The gospel, fixed in definition and flexible in demonstration, is *scattered* to the world . . . and *smothered* with love.

WHEN HOPE SPRINGS A LEAK INSTEAD OF ETERNAL

The year was 1805. Thomas Jefferson was elected president, Susan Lucci lost her first chance to be nominated for a Daytime Emmy, John Kerry and George W. Bush began campaigning for president, and the media coverage began for the 2005 Super Bowl. Of course I am kidding! Everyone knows Jefferson was elected in 1804.

However, the biggest event of 1804 was the Lewis&Clark.com expedition, sponsored by Pepsi. Their task was to find a route to the Northwest Territory and claim it for the United States before Bill Gates could. They set out from St. Louis in May of 1804. Being typical males, they got lost and did not stop for directions until they hit North Dakota sometime in November, where they found assistance in a young Shoshone girl named Pocahontas, which in English means "Sacajawea." These men lived on hope . . . mainly hoping they would never again spend two years on a keelboat with a bunch of musty-smelling men and no ESPN.

The Lewis&Clark.com expedition paved the way for a flood of people leaving the hurricane season of the East Coast, only to discover the tornadoes and Indians of Kansas. These people became known in history books as hearty pioneers, because behind every hearty pioneer man, there was a hearty pioneer woman, usually with a sour look on her hearty face and seven kids under her hearty arms. They would be linebackers in today's NFL.

They were people who would boil water, wash clothes, bathe children, and cook supper, all in the same kettle . . . without ever changing the water. It is a process still used today in truck stops everywhere. These hearty pioneers lived by one motto: "He who uses the same kettle to wash clothes and cook food, and lives in a mud shack with seven children and no air freshener, will never smile in a group picture."

You do not have to look very far to see people today who are struggling to find their way in a difficult land. They seem to be in a hopeless situation, reaching out with no one offering hope. In trying times the voice of the doomsdayers and the naysayers sing their loudest songs, while those who know the song of hope remain insensitively silent.

As Christians we should continually be singing the song of hope because of Christ. Yet when our song should be "I Stand Amazed in the Presence," it all too frequently fades into "I Stand in a Maze, Where Is Your Presence?" It seems to me if we expect to navigate through the troubled waters of hopeless situations, we need to plug a few spiritual leaks. While we are at it, we probably need to change our tune.

THE ROAD TO ENLIGHTENMENT OFTEN PASSES THROUGH MAYBERRY

Once upon a time, I played softball. In fact, it was remarkable how softly I played. People used to travel from all over my imagination just to watch me play. When I slid, I stirred up enough dust to cover Oklahoma, and that was just getting out of the car. My fans under the stands would scream and yell my name every time I headed for the outfield. They usually stopped screaming when I went back to the dugout to get my pants and glove.

My nickname was almost "The Babe." That would have been disrespectful of Babe Ruth, so I was "The Boob," which was awfully close. (Out of all the names they called me, it is the only one printable.) On that rare occasion when I would make contact with the ball, I would hear it say, "What was that? I thought I felt something." I hit so many ground balls that as soon as I stepped up to the plate, worms would hide their young. There was one game when I was legitimately cheered. I was the eighth player, and my presence at the game kept us from forfeiting. It felt great to be needed.

The second episode of the *Andy Griffith Show* centered on Opie's first meeting with Aunt Bea. Rose had been taking care of Opie, but she got married and moved. Enter Aunt Bea. She could not do anything as well as Rose. She tried really hard, even trying to learn how to swing a baseball bat like Rose. Things just didn't work out, and Aunt Bea decided to move on.

Aunt Bea and Andy were outside at the car saying good-bye, unaware that Opie was watching and listening from his upstairs window. Finally, he could not stand it any longer and ran downstairs, out the door, and yelled for Aunt Bea not to leave. Andy was caught completely by surprise and asked Opie what changed his mind. Opie responded, "Well, if she goes, what will happen to her? She doesn't know how to do anything—play baseball, catch fish, or hunt frogs! She'll be helpless! So that's why she's gotta stay, so I can teach 'em to her!" Opie then hugged Aunt Bea and said, "You need me!"

On the road to Damascus, the apostle Paul was blinded by a light and met Jesus. In his first letter to the church at Corinth, he wrote that the church is like a body, all the parts dependent upon each other. The body cannot function properly if any part is not doing its job, and no part is more important than the other.

On the road to Mayberry, I was blinded by a light, but mine was in the form of a six-year-old character on a television show. Sometimes light shines where we least expect it. I didn't meet

Jesus, but I did discover a theology of need. You see, not everyone in the church can play baseball, catch fish, or hunt frogs, but we can learn from each other. We are all part of the same body—and we need each other with our different gifts. That is the gospel according to Paul . . . and Opie.

Chapter 8:
If You Think You've Got Problems, Consider the Person Who Had to Clean the Ark

Lessons on Servanthood

A Pilgrim's Progress Is Always Measured by His Bunions

horrible movement is sweeping our country and leaving unsightly straw everywhere. We seem to be infatuated (emphasis on the "fat") with fitness. On any given cable channel, you can find Stepford Wives–like women advertising the latest torture device under the guise of exercise equipment. No matter which machine they are advertising, these women always look perfect and never sweat. The unsweaty women are especially unnerving during aerobics infomercials.

Aerobics is not for the unsweaty woman. It is best described as an activity where women try to out-ugly one another in outfits designed by a committee that never met, while jumping, kicking, grunting, and generally flailing about the room in what looks like some form of ritualistic dance involving distressed ostriches. There are people who combine aerobics with karate and boxing into one workout. If I tried it, I would spontaneously combust.

The years 1979 to 1983 were an important ten years for me because of two things: I tried exercising, and I discovered I had a slight math problem. I kept fit during those early years of marriage because I took the minister's words seriously when he said something about "Till girth do us part" and "Gentlemen, start your engines." (He was also the chaplain at the local racetrack.) My mother-in-law then waved the caution flag, and Beverly and I left for our honeymoon.

I don't exercise anymore. I have too many body parts that could unnecessarily explode. My idea of fitness is to sit in my recliner, drink a diet soda, and eat unsalted pork skins while bench-pressing my Chihuahuas. It does not do me much good, but when I forget to close the blinds, it sure gives the neighbors an interesting picture.

In those early years of exercising, I had callus-hardened hands from lifting weights and bunion-infested feet from running. There is an important rule of callused-thumb in exercising—it does not take long for some insensitive member of the bunion family to attach itself to the parts of your body that endure the most contact.

That same principle applies to spiritual exercise. If you want to measure your spiritual progress, there are a few important questions you should answer. Are your hands callused from lifting up a brother or from tearing him down? Are your feet blistered from walking a mile in a brother's shoes or from walking on him? Are your fingers sore from turning the pages of your Bible for daily guidance or from searching for a text to prove a point?

CHAPTER 8: Lessons on Servanthood

Are your arms weary from wrapping them around a hurting friend or from holding on to yourself? Does your jaw ache from giving out continuous praise or from dishing out constant criticism? Are your eyes tired from looking at life like Jesus would or from adjusting to the blinders?

In our Christian pilgrimage, we all have spiritual bunions . . . our progress is measured by how we got them.

LET'S TURN IN OUR HYMNBOOKS TO "THERE'S POWER IN THE TOWEL"

I can remember being the ruler of the entire sixth-grade class at Fair Park Elementary School in Little Rock, Arkansas. I could run faster, jump higher, and had prettier hair than any of my buddies in the sixth grade. I was in charge, and everyone knew it (except my parents—for some reason, I never could convince them).

With the pastor away this week, that leaves me in charge of the church office—which is just the church administrator and me. I told her to get me a cup of coffee, and she just laughed. I stepped on her bad foot. She will never laugh again.

I haven't felt this kind of power since I turned down a one-million-dollar-a-year baseball contract with the Yankees to become a youth minister. I feel very powerful. I may organize some Goodwill Games for the United States to compete against Communist Texas. I may even do the ultimate: get Beverly to dye her hair, give one of my Chihuahuas a trumpet, and form my own Christian television network. But that probably wouldn't work. Think about it. Can you name one bald TV evangelist?

All of these thoughts were going through my mind while I was sitting in my oval office Tuesday. What could I do with all of this self-appointed authority? I thought about bringing in a faith healer to grow me some hair, but I've never seen one with that much faith. I even thought about making it mandatory that every Christian tithe, but in the same breath, I thought about getting blood out of the proverbial turnip.

For one passing moment, I considered adding a new bylaw to the church constitution that simply requires every church member to be nice. Finally, I thought about ordering everyone in the church to adopt a servant attitude. Then it hit me. If we have to be ordered to be servants, then we aren't really servants, are we?

That line of thought trickled down to me and my power, and it spread to images of people in our church and in other churches who think they are to rule the church. I knew where that line of thought was going, but I couldn't stop it. It took me right into the face of Jesus as He washed the feet of the disciples.

I realized then that the secret to power for any church, with or without a pastor, is wrapped up in servanthood. We know that there is power in the blood and power in the Cross, but there is also power in servanthood.

What we as Christians need to do is stop staring at the Cross . . . and start searching for a towel.

There's More Than One Way to Trim the Fat

Part of my job description, as I see it, is to be the moral and spiritual watchdog in my church and force the members to believe as I do on every controversial issue that may exist in our universe. With that in mind, there is a movement underfoot (or should I say underfat?) to rid our nation of all fat content—with the exception of the irritating man in the beer commercial who coined the phrase "Whazzup?"

I may not look like it, but I have tasted many fat-free foods. Like a person who would wear a tank top and sweatpants to a wedding or bring store-bought food to a potluck dinner, most fat-free foods have no taste. I am very familiar with no taste. I pick out my own clothes, and I ate youth-camp meat loaf for twenty-five years.

CHAPTER 8: Lessons on Servanthood

If a food tastes good, it will ooze fat. If it sits on the counter long enough, it will just ooze. My grandmother was a wonderful cook. We always had plenty of fried chicken, fried potatoes, fried pork chops, and bacon. We called her the Wizard of Ooze.

According to my doctor, my annual fat intake is somewhere in the neighborhood of the gross tonnage of a Winnebago. My cholesterol goes up just watching Porky Pig cartoons, and dogs follow me everywhere because they think I'm bacon. There are good reasons that this is not healthy, but I will use reasons that are totally fabricated.

Once food travels through our digestive system and its luggage arrives from Cleveland, it explodes and lands in all areas of our bodies. The fat globules immediately congregate together and head straight for the blood. They just sit there getting fatter and fatter, causing all sorts of trouble (the fat globules, not the politicians).

In some instances, the fat globules actually replace the brain. This is most evident in the Crocodile Hunter and mimes. If the globules stay long enough to form committees, they can block the flow of blood to and from the heart, one of our more important organs.

As bad as all of this seems, there is something worse. It is those of us who have become spiritually fat and are not doing anything to lighten the load. We find ourselves in that condition by taking everything in and not giving anything out. This condition is usually caused by our lack of personal stewardship of time, gifts, and money.

Each of us knows what we ought to be doing in the area of stewardship. The problem is that sometimes we become so spiritually fat from a lack of spiritual exercise, we begin to suffer from a hardening of the "oughteries." We know what we ought to do, but we seldom do it. When we reach that point, the answer can only be found within ourselves, in communication with God, the Great Dietician.

To put it simply . . . all oughteries lead to the heart.

THE CHICKEN MAY HAVE CROSSED THE ROAD, BUT HE DIDN'T CROW ABOUT IT

Two disturbing newspaper articles have me concerned and have ruffled my feathers. The first article informed me that chickens are roaming free in Key West, Florida. Although some are having difficulty with addition and subtraction, they are multiplying at an alarming rate. With Key West being an island, the chickens have no natural enemies, like foxes or Colonel Sanders, but there are ordinances protecting them from chicken harassment, particularly from degrading chicken puns.

The residents are trying to keep abreast of the situation but just do not have a leg to stand on. Unless you come at them with a fajita skillet and a flour tortilla, chickens are not normally aggressive. These chickens are evidently descendants of fighting roosters, some of them still wearing their boxing gloves.

Washington has responded by sending representatives to conduct surveys and appoint committees, but it seems to be just an excuse to use their frequent-fryer miles.

As if the rise in sales of rap music and the increasing popularity of reality-based television shows weren't enough to make me queasy, I read another newspaper article, which described the declining population of the lesser prairie chicken. Why scientists are concerned about this is beyond me. Doesn't the term *lesser* imply that there aren't going to be very many anyway?

For you who are avianically challenged, a lesser prairie chicken is a small grouse. (I once knew a small grouse. He kept to himself. Didn't have many friends. Complained a lot. He became a lawyer.) It has a distinct look, with two pointy appendages sticking up out of its head (the prairie chicken, not the lawyer). It looks very much like a cross between a Chihuahua and a punk rocker. (Actually, that could describe a prairie chicken or a lawyer.) The decreasing population of the lesser prairie chicken is evidently a problem with their habitat, the lesser prairie, also known as Kansas.

I feel sorry for the chicken. Nobody likes to be lesser. We have great-grandparents, Great Plains, Great Divide, Great Lakes, and the Great Wall of China. Could F. Scott Fitzgerald have sold a book with the title, *The Lesser Gatsby*? Would any Greek in his right mind follow a leader named Alexander the Lesser? There is less-filling beer, but even the commercial says it tastes great.

Nobody likes to be lesser, and that is why the words of Jesus grate on us sometimes. He said it best in Luke 9:48: "The least among all of you is the greatest" (NRSV). Jesus spent His time ministering to the lesser crowd, not crowing about His achievements. We should not worry about the pecking order of which one is the greatest.

In our efforts to be lesser Christians, we must be bold. We cannot afford to be chicken.

WE ARE THE SALT OF THE EARTH, BUT SOME OF US NEED A LID ON OUR SHAKER

As far as I'm concerned, the ingredients for a fine dinner begin with the main course. Read the following instructions and guess what I am describing: Twist off the claws. Crack each claw with a nutcracker. Separate the tailpiece from the body by arching the back until it cracks. (Hint: I went through this process in college to remove a surprised cat from my leg.) Actually, this describes part of the process for correctly eating a lobster. I simply left out the massive sucking noises.

I never eat anything for which the instructions include Open the remaining part of the body by cracking sideways. I want to eat my food, not perform an autopsy on it. To properly eat lobster, you must have access to a bib, lemon, clarified butter (I prefer confused butter), a shell cracker, and a lobster fork. That is more equipment than David used to face Goliath. The bib is to give protection from the "wonderful juices that burst forth from the recesses." Call me wacky, but I don't want my table food bursting forth from any recesses.

Just by reading the instructions, one of the strangest dishes you will ever prepare is sauerkraut. Does this sound enticing? "Place a layer of thinly shredded cabbage in a stone crock . . . sprinkle lightly with noniodized salt . . . pound vigorously with a wooden stomper." That sounds like a gourmet dinner at a tractor pull.

It continues: "Place a board on top and place something on the board to weigh it down." That, of course, will keep the sauerkraut from escaping if it becomes violent from being pounded. Here's the kicker: "Set in a warm place to ferment. After about six days, remove the scum that has formed on top." Again, call me wacky, but since Beverly's first two or three meals, I just don't eat anything that requires scum removal.

Remembering how the sauerkraut was cooked, try this recipe for meatball glaze: "1 cup sauerkraut, 1 cup cranberry sauce, 8 oz. bottle chili sauce." It's not good for the stomach, but it would be perfect for bricking a driveway, killing the Loch Ness monster, or lubing an Abrams A1 tank.

God has prepared a great banquet and everyone is invited. The cooking is done, the table is set, and the main course is the Bread of Life. The only problem is we have spent so much time arguing over the menu or who sits at the head table that we have gotten behind on delivering personal invitations to His feast. Not everyone is going to accept, and we must be careful how we ask.

It only takes a pinch of salt to make food pleasing to the

palate. We are to be the salt of the earth, but when others see us as holier-than-thou, we have used too much salt and ruined their appetite for spiritual food. If we ever get around to offering the invitation, it falls on deaf ears and hungry hearts.

The key to the number of people at God's banquet depends on our knowing the difference between being salt . . . and being salty.

To Be a Good Samaritan, You Must First Get Rid of Pride and Prejudice

In high school and college, I was fascinated by literature. I especially liked the classics like *Catcher in the Rye* (about a Jewish baseball player), *A Farewell to Arms* (about an Italian chef and a bizarre cooking accident), *Archie Comics*, and *Cliffs Notes*. Lessons learned from literature have stayed with me. *Animal Farm* taught me how to be a youth minister. *War and Peace* helped prepare me for church business meetings.

Robert Louis Stevenson's classic, *Dr. Jekyll and Mr. Hyde*, prepared me for dealing with the many mood swings of my own teenagers. *Moby Dick* has helped over the years whenever I have tried to harpoon a whale, and Homer's *Iliad* comes to mind every time I have to deal with a slow-witted Greek named Ajax. Finally, who could forget Satan's associate, Beelzebubba, from John Milton's *Paradise Lost in Alabama*?

To fully appreciate great literature, we must understand certain terms. *Baroque* is a literary style that is without flaw, as in the statement, "If it ain't baroque, don't fix it." The *Baconian theory* is a theory that someone other than Shakespeare wrote his works while eating pork. *Carpe diem* is a phrase coined in Arkansas that means "That carp is dead." *Coda* is a brief addition in the middle of a biblical passage, as in the phrase "Joseph and his coda many colors."

Bucolic describes a quiet, pastoral story about sick babies, and a *closed couplet* is a husband and wife with no friends. A *signifier* is a concrete sign that evokes an abstract idea, as in the statement "Remember, only you can prevent signifiers." A *canto,* in a literary argument using incorrect grammar, is the opposite of *cannot.* The *setting* is the natural background of a story set in any Southern state, as in the sentence "They was setting over there by that possum."

Another masterful piece of literature is the parable of the good Samaritan. It has melodrama, plot, characters, and a narrator. To fully appreciate its meaning, we must come to terms with its intent. The main question in this parable is not "Who is my neighbor?" but "To whom can I be a neighbor?" That's the trouble with parables. They were meant to be verbs, not nouns.

For some of us, being kind to a hurting friend would be like entering a brave new world. It is always easier to pass by on the other side, even if it is a hallway at church. We are supposed to have a heart like Christ, not a heart of darkness. We all have hurts and needs that can be helped by the outstretched hand of a Christian brother or sister.

Even the scarlet letter fades into oblivion against the backdrop of the blood of Christ.

WHEN GOD GETS A HOLD ON YOU, IT'S SHAKE, RATTLE, AND RULE

L et's look at the word *shake* and its impact on America. Early in our history, we had a group of people who acquired an irritating twitch during a three-month voyage on a ship with only one bathroom and were extremely nervous upon their arrival in a foreign land. They were called Shakers. Those who resorted to foul language were referred to as "salty Shakers."

Several years later a German immigrant in Pennsylvania, Ben Holstein, stood by in horror as one of his dairy cows got caught on a high-speed treadmill and invented the milkshake. Normal folks in the colonies could not afford plumbers, so they built wells to get water from natural springs. Every Saturday night people from nearby farms would gather at a friend's well and shake it furiously for an hour. Thus was born the phrase "Shake well before using."

In the 1950s and '60s, we listened to songs like "Shake, Rattle, and Roll" and "A Whole Lotta Shakin' Goin' On." Then we watched in screaming wonder as Elvis squirmed, fidgeted, and gyrated to "I'm All Shook Up." In the 1970s we barely survived intelligence-mocking disco music and were encouraged by KC and The Sunshine Band to dance to songs like "Shake Your Booty." I, being a good Baptist, listened to Lawrence Welk and shook nothing more than my bubble bath.

In school we studied Shakespeare, and when we went fishing, we used Shakespeare fishing equipment, from which we got the phrase "A bass! A bass! My kingdom for a bass!" We are told to "shake a leg," "shake it off," and at the end of the wedding ceremony, the minister tells us to "shake hands and come out fighting." Sadly, we are "shaken" by horrifying experiences such as professional basketball players with purple hair.

Several years ago I stood in a pecan grove and watched a tractor with a giant set of pliers grab hold of a pecan tree, apparently because it had been misbehaving, and shake it violently. Everything fell out, including leaves, pecans, bark, Isaac Newton, and a small furry animal with a deer-in-the-headlights look on his face. My first thought was that I hoped Beverly never got a tractor like that.

A more humbling concern was if God had a similar tractor. Sometimes it takes a good shaking to get our attention. It may be the words of a friend or a verse of Scripture at the right time, but God has a way of shaking us up and rattling some things around before He can rule in our lives.

Until we have been shaken by God, we really do not know the meaning of the word.

THE TREE, THEN THE TOMB, THEN THE TOWEL:
A GOD-INSPIRED SEQUENCE ON INDEPENDENCE DAY

We all know the heartwarming story of how fireworks were invented. Two Baptists were rubbed together in the early tenth century. Ha! Ha! Just kidding! Everyone knows Baptists weren't invented until the King James Bible was published. Actually, a cook in rural China was toiling in the kitchen and mixed some ingredients together that were better left unacquainted.

The ensuing catastrophe was history's first man-made explosion of sparks. Historians are unsure what the Chinese cook was trying to create, although they knew he would have to eat it again in two hours.

The association of fireworks and Independence Day goes back to the Revolutionary War. American soldiers were on the verge of victory in a battle and began putting down their firearms. "No! No! Bad gun!" "Your mother wears combat boots!" "You've got a problem: you're always loaded!" Cooler heads prevailed, and instead of putting them down, they began firing them into the air in a celebrative spirit. Years later, while they were passing time at the old soldiers' home, it dawned on them that the war would have ended much sooner had they actually fired their muskets into the British.

There was another lesson learned through this experience. Encouraged by their wives, it took the soldiers about sixty seconds to realize that firing their muskets into the air probably would have gone over better outdoors. For that they became known as Minutemen, and firing small arms became a standard celebration for the Fourth of July.

This continued into the nineteenth century, when a few misguided people in California misunderstood the concept and began firing small legs. Another slight adjustment to the celebration happened in the 1960s when the hippie culture decided to eliminate the middleman and simply believed fireworks were going off inside their heads.

How do you celebrate your Independence Day? You see, for the lost person, Independence Day comes the day he accepts the free gift of God's grace through Jesus, forever freeing him from the bondage of sin. What about the Christian? Our Independence Day comes the day we begin to serve God, not because of what we can gain but out of obedience to Him. Christianity does not end with the Cross and the tomb—it begins.

The most appropriate symbol of the New Testament is a towel, symbolic of our Lord washing the feet of the disciples, the perfect picture of servanthood ... and freedom. Do we have a servant's heart? If we "have done it unto one of the least of these my brethren" (Matthew 25:40 KJV), we have done it unto Jesus. Celebrate your independence. Serve others; serve God.

The Cross is gone, the tomb is empty ... but the towel is waiting.

IF YOU'RE LOOKING FOR A SIGN FROM ABOVE, CHECK OUT THE SON

We are all familiar with signs and symbols. If you drive in Nashville, you know an orange traffic cone means that stretch of road will be under construction until your current first-grader graduates from college. Some people know under which sign they were born. I wish I had been born in a bakery so when people ask me about my sign, I could respond, "Delivered fresh every day!"

Signs are important to baseball players. Watch the third-base coach and see if he doesn't act as if a swarm of bees is eating Mexican food inside his shirt.

Signs are also important to parents. When Beverly and I had our first baby, we knew it was time to change her diaper when our Chihuahua would roll over on his back, cover his nose, and start howling uncontrollably.

If I see a clear plastic covering over a doorway with a sign

185

marked Quarantined, I know I have discovered the entrance to Meredith's room. A good sign for her to be born under would have been Garage Sale.

In my travels I have come across many interesting signs. Did you know there is a Dull, Tennessee, and a Brilliant, Alabama? Are you familiar with Perry, Tennessee, and Como, Tennessee? I have been through Harrah, Oklahoma, and Bellafonte, Arkansas. I have also been through Octa, Missouri. Each year they receive an Academy Award for Best Octa.

I have crossed over the Forked Deer River. I personally have never seen a forked deer. I saw a sign at one business advertising Fast Gas. (Carefully insert your own punch line here.) One ranch in Kansas was selling Polled Herefords. How do you poll a Hereford? The easiest way is to stand at the precinct exit and interview them when they finish voting.

The most endearing sign for a Christian, besides Honk If You Love Jesus, is a cross. That is understandable, to a point. I have always liked the idea of a manger or a tomb as the symbol for Christianity, but then the Crusaders in the twelfth century would have looked like a bunch of wimps if they had gone into battle with a manger or tomb emblazoned on their chest.

These are important signs for Christians, but they miss the area where Jesus spent most of His time—serving people. The most appropriate sign of a servant in the New Testament is the towel. You see, the manger, the cross, and the tomb require no effort on our part. The towel does. We must be servants. In sign terminology we must *stop* thinking of ourselves, *yield* to God's will, and *go* serve others before we *exit* this life.

We may not know under which sign we were born, but we had better decide under which sign we will live.

lesson 80

MORE THAN A WATER POT

I thought it was going to be another ordinary day. At about noon my owner picked me up for our daily trip to the well. She was very good to me, if only because she had never thrown me at one of her husbands. Most of the women went to the well around sunset, talked with each other, and made a social occasion out of it. Not my owner. Her reputation in the community was less than admirable with the other women. As she walked, her eyes searched left and right for any of the local gossipers.

When we got close enough to see the well, she stopped so suddenly that I thought she would drop me. Strangely enough there was a man sitting there—a Jew at that! Now I may be just a water pot, but I knew we were about to have an awkward situation. (You see, Jews and Samaritans had hated each other for several hundred years.)

CHAPTER 8: Lessons on Servanthood

When we reached the well, instead of degrading her, the Jew asked my owner for a drink. He was not only being nice to a Samaritan, but He was talking to a woman! I figured this guy just fell off the sandal wagon or He knew something we did not. It took her completely by surprise because she simply could not imagine a Jewish man talking to a Samaritan woman.

As they began to talk, the Jew told her she could have living water—if she drank it she would never thirst again. Well, I certainly had never heard of such a thing, and I knew she was too sharp to buy into it either. Then He said something that changed the whole tone of the conversation. He told her to go call her husband. When she said she did not have a husband, He said she was right—in fact, she had already had five husbands, and the man she was living with was not one of them. Wow! I knew He was either a prophet or had taken a slow walk through one too many vineyards.

They talked about worship, and I could tell my owner's attitude was beginning to change. Finally, she told Him she knew the Messiah was coming and He would straighten everything out. I thought that would end the conversation, she would fill me up, and we would be on our way. Boy, was I wrong. He looked at her with the most sincere eyes I have seen and said, "I who speak to you am He." That put her over the edge, and she took off like a scalded donkey. She ran to the village and told everyone that she had seen the Messiah.

From the look on her face, I could tell that because of this man, she would never be the same, and I realized that we now had something in common. She had become what I had been all these years . . . a vessel in the hands of the Master.

Chapter 9:

It's Not Christ's Shoes That Are Hard to Fill; It's the Holes in His Hands

Lessons from the Example of Christ

You Can Find Anything at Wal-Mart, Including Elvis and Jesus

You may not have noticed, but August is one of our more holiday-impaired months. To combat this lack of planning on the part of our forefathers, I decided to do something celebratory. I had a brain lapse the size of Idaho and went to opening day at a new Wal-Mart Supercenter.

It was everything a soccer riot dreams about being when it grows up. Except for changing my first dirty diaper, it was the most stomach-turning, tension-filled, blood pressure–raising, nausea-inducing ninety minutes of my life. Then I found a parking place and went inside.

Before I could enter the inner sanctum, the first thing I had to do was get past the much-too-happy and smile-too-big-for-her-face former prison guard at the front trying to force me to take a buggy. Once I convinced her I did not need one, I felt like calling a cab to get from one end of the store to the other. Now I know how a Chihuahua feels in the Astrodome.

I had not seen so much stuff since our last garage sale. The Wal-Mart Supercenter had everything I didn't know I needed until I got there. I was so entranced I almost bought some deodorant featuring the slogan "So effective you could skip a day." I resisted. With all of my aches and pains from being the oldest person on our church softball team, I figured if I tried skipping for a whole day, I would get injured.

With cunning survival skills learned from years of shopping on the day after Thanksgiving, I carefully made my way to the Elvis Presley display in the electronics section. We may celebrate our independence in July, but August has "International Elvis Week," commemorating the anniversary of the death of the real king of rock-'n'-roll. (He beat out Chubby Checker for the title simply because no one would take seriously a king named Chubby, although we did have a president named Rutherford.)

When Elvis walked into a room, girls screamed. In my younger days, girls screamed whenever I walked into a room, but they usually calmed down after I washed off my acne cream. Through Elvis impersonators and Elvis sightings, Elvis Presley is as popular today as he was years ago. I have never personally made an Elvis sighting, although I once had a sixty-five-year old secretary named Rosie who did a great Elvis impersonation. The closest I've ever been to the king of rock-'n'-roll is my wife calling me Chubby.

The hoopla over the opening of Wal-Mart and the events surrounding Elvis did inspire me to compare his life to that of another King. One king lived in a mansion called Graceland.

This King is preparing a mansion for us, built on grace. One king died and, contrary to what some may believe, is still dead. This King died and, contrary to what some may believe, rose from the dead after three days.

On the anniversary of one king's death, the day is filled with mourning. On the anniversary of this King's death, joy comes in the morning. One king is gone. This King is coming. People claim to see one king all the time. God only knows if people see the King of kings in us.

I, too, am a fan of the king of rock-'n'-roll. More importantly, I am a child of the King who rolled the rock away. It was He who wrote the Song of Life and I, for one, will forever be indebted to His Music.

Elvis had some great music, but Elvis has left the building. Jesus is still here, singing His Song. Our job, as followers of the King, is to increase the number of listeners.

DOES THE COMMAND TO LOVE INCLUDE THINGS THAT SLURP IN THE NIGHT?

I do not like confrontation. I even cringe when one of my Chihuahuas talks back to me or when my wife challenges my particular hairstyle of the day. There is a subject that Oprah's producers refuse to discuss, and it is more volatile than the squeezing-the-toothpaste-from-the-middle-of-the-tube controversy. But I must take a stand, because it is a subject that is on everyone's breath: eating crawdads.

These creatures were not mentioned in a television movie about Noah's Ark, which was so careful about details that it included the story of David and Goliath sharing a life raft. I believe it was the same movie that showed Louis Armstrong blowing his trumpet and bringing down the malls of Jericho.

Eating crawdads is something that should be attempted by mature adults who have no class and no access to sharp objects.

CHAPTER 9: Lessons from the Example of Christ

I am a trained professional. As a parent I have pulled thousands of disgusting objects out of jean pockets and have had the good sense not to eat half of them.

For you who are crustaceously challenged, let me update you on a few facts. Crawdads have five pairs of legs, two pairs of feelers, stalked eyes, and gills. Many of them came to earth in the 1990s as disgruntled friends on *Jerry Springer*.

The first step in crawdad dining is to pull off the head. Then you extract the meat with your mouth through a series of intensely severe sucking sounds that exude atmosphere and spark romantic conversation in restaurants, such as the following:

Wife: "Honey, did you hear that noise? It sounded like five thousand people walking through deep mud while trying to stuff Jell-O into a concerned goose."

Husband: "Ha! Ha! It's just that large man in the next booth eating crawdads."

Personally, I have a simple digestive rule whereby I never eat anything that squishes or has the potential to become the subject of another Peter Benchley novel.

My usual reaction to disgusting food is to flee. Crawdads easily qualify, and I have never even tasted one. There is a parallel here to life because we often approach certain groups of people (fill in your own blank) with the same kind of love, respect, and compassion we usually reserve for crawdads. We make assumptions on outward appearance and never take the time to get to know them.

Did you know crawdads are mostly found in shallow water? It is almost like they want to be caught, like they want somebody to find them. Jesus had a way with unlovely or unwanted people. He could cut through their hard outer shells and get right to their hearts, without biting off their heads.

Being fishers of men is not so difficult . . . it's the crawdads of life that take extra effort.

WHEN DID CAESAR BECOME A SALAD AND JEREMIAH A BULLFROG?

D o you ever get the feeling that life in the new millennium is a NASCAR 500 race and you're driving a '49 Plymouth? It hit me when I read another article about those pesky research scientists. Do you think they are researching life-changing questions like "Why do so many sweet potatoes look like Richard Nixon?" or "Will a suddenly jolted cow give cottage cheese?" Of course not! They held a conference on medical terminology and decided to change the names of some of our body parts in order to make the medical language more universal.

With a universal parts language, doctors from all over the world can operate on me and tell internationally humorous body-membrane stories during surgery . . . without having to point.

First doctor: "Hey, Fred! Did you hear the one about the

Baptist, the Methodist, and the ipsilateral aorta going to heaven?"

Second doctor: "Oh no! I dropped my gum!"

I just want the language to be simple so I will know what the doctor is talking about when he looks at my blood and says my triceratops are high.

Here are a few examples of the changes: Your elbow is now your *cubitus*, which could also mean you have just been bitten by a square Latin dog. The end of the small intestine is the *papilla ileal*, which comes from the Italian word for "sick pillow."

The Adam's apple is now the *laryngeal prominence*, which sounds more like a pope with a throat problem. If you have high cheekbones or "Northern" cheekbones, you now have a *zygoma*. Conversely, if you have low cheekbones or "Southern" cheekbones, you have a *Zygoma Pyle*.

Why couldn't they change the "funny bone" to the "if-you-hit-this-puppy-just-right-it-will-hurt-like-heck bone"? With all of the name changes, my primordial need is to be assured that during a routine operation to remove my tonsils, someone doesn't sneeze and take out my uvula.

Even with the changes, life goes on. In the restaurant business, Caesar is now a salad. In the music culture of the 1970s and '80s, ABBA was not Father, Madonna was not Mother Mary, and Jeremiah was a bullfrog. But in our fast-paced contemporary world, there is still one name that means the same as it did two thousand years ago . . . Jesus. And as the song reminds us, "there's something about that name." He continues to be Master, Savior, Lord; and His name still calls to mind words like *love*, *patience*, *kindness*, and *forgiveness*.

CHAPTER 9: Lessons from the Example of Christ

Too bad we can't say the same thing about the term *Christian*. The word is supposed to mean "Christlike." But these days, when *Christian* is mentioned, too many negative images are brought to mind. When did *Christian* become a bad word? I can't put a specific date on it, but it happens to us when we live our lives too far away from words like *love, joy, peace, patience, kindness, goodness, gentleness,* and *self-control.*

Is there something about *your* name? If you are going to call yourself a Christian . . . there is.

THERE IS ONLY ONE WAY TO GOD, AND IT IS NOT MILKY

According to a survey of eleven hundred people, 59 percent of adults believe there is intelligent life in outer space. Of course, those same people believe there is intelligent life in Washington, D.C. Except for a high-school friend who was from another planet, I am not that familiar with outer space. However, there was one girl in college who liked snuff, and we nicknamed her "The Big Dipper." Other than that, my knowledge of things spacey is limited to roller-derby cheerleaders.

Raising two children from Mars, I do know that Mars is named after the Roman god of candy bars and will be fading in brightness over the next few years. But then, so will many of us. As I look around, I notice several have already begun. Deimos, one of the moons of Mars, rises and sets twice a day, just like my Chihuahuas. Another fact about Mars is that UFO sightings are at their greatest number during those times when Mars is closest to earth, and very often when a cheap bottle of wine is closest to mouth.

Like questionable dishes at a potluck dinner, space has some unexplained phenomena. It takes six hours for light to travel to earth, sometimes longer, depending on the number of orange traffic cones along the way. Modern science museums have areas, similar to the old Star Trek television series, where you can simulate beaming in and out from one planet to another ... just like schoolteachers during faculty meetings.

Another strange event is watching a meteor shower. (They are shy, so don't look when you hand them their towel.) A passing comet, like a herd of teenagers passing through a pizza place, leaves debris everywhere. The falling debris creates a showering effect, hence the term *meteor shower* ... not to be confused with the carnage from a bridal shower. Very bright meteors are called fireballs and are placed in advanced classes at school. They are smart but still have to be told to shower.

A more familiar event is a solar eclipse. This is when the moon comes between earth and the sun, blocking the sunlight from reaching earth. It could be a partial eclipse or a total eclipse. Either way, the moon is preventing the sun from doing what it was designed to do, give warmth and light.

As Christians we sometimes let things come between Jesus and us. It could be a job, money, a relationship, or even a power trip. We could even have a personal agenda for our church instead of praying for God's leadership. When that happens, we cut off God's light and create partial or total spiritual darkness for ourselves.

The worst thing that could happen to one's heart would be a total eclipse of the Son.

WHEN IT COMES TO THE BREAD OF LIFE, DON'T LOAF AROUND

Thanks to a recent newspaper article, my children have been exposed to beans. Evidently, the bean cuisine movement is shaking our country. One bean recipe was called Five-Layer Dip. When I was in high school, a five-layer dip was an extreme nerd, which meant *two* pocket protectors. Mine was a Mr. Peanut.

Another recipe was called Bean Dip Trio. Wasn't that a music group in the 1960s? I think they played at my prom, because I remember the DJ saying, "And now, seniors, grab your parents and let's dance to the music of the *Bean Dip Trio*." Man, it was a gas!

There were also articles on grits and sausage. *Grits* is a term short for *hominy grits,* as in the phrase "You sing melody and I'll sing hominy." According to the article, "Chefs are now taking humble grits and using them in enticing ways." My kids are already dealing with people wearing plaid shirts with striped pants. I don't want them enticed by grits.

The article referred to a grits blueberry soufflé as a "creamy and puffed concoction." I had a puffed concoction once but immediately went to the doctor to have it removed.

In closing this horrible culinary nightmare, let me give you a few words of warning about a sausage called "head cheese." According to one article, it is "composed of small pieces of hog's head bound in gelatin and seasoned with white wine." I am not a drinker, but if I were going to purposely eat small pieces of hog's head bound in gelatin, *I* would have to be seasoned with white wine.

In this country we seem to be infatuated by food. When you consider the time it takes to make the shopping list, do the shopping, study recipes, and cook the food, we spend more time being consumed by the thought of food than we do actually consuming it. This would especially be true if I were to consume hog's head sausage, because I would have to think about it for a week. For a politician it would be the ultimate pork barrel.

Jesus told the crowd not to work for food that spoils, but for food that endures. A few verses later, He refers to Himself as "the bread of life" (John 6:35). Obviously, we need food to survive physically. Jesus is simply telling us that instead of being overly concerned about consuming food, we should concentrate our lives on being consumed by the Bread of Life.

DON'T BELIEVE EVERYTHING
YOU HEAR . . . OR READ

low the http.com.trumpets, and turn out the color org.net.guard, because like a largemouth bass on a deep-running lure, I am online! After several angst-filled hours, I have discovered that the e in "e-mail" stands for extremely exasperating experience. In one moment of frustration, I almost went to the suggested "navigation bar," but I was afraid I would not be able to walk out unassisted.

I am not an alarmist, but while I was browsing, I learned something very disturbing. Our world is being attacked by spam. Please do not frighten the children, but unless you listen to a lot of Jimi Hendrix records, this is probably news. Except for a bizarre experiment with crawdad fajitas and one quick trip to a discount sushi bar, I have never been overly concerned about an attack from food. I dread thinking my epitaph could read, "Here lies Martin Babb; he was gentle as a lamb. We thought he died from natural causes, but the autopsy said, 'death by spam.'"

There is hope. My instructions included a section entitled "Tips for Fighting Spam" and an antispam tutorial. As soon as I discovered this Orson Welles–like War of the Wired spam scare, I went straight for the tutored spam and found the origin of spam and ways to avoid getting spam.

I learned that the people who send spam are called spammers, and they harvest it right there on my computer. With everything else growing in my office, the last thing I need is a spam crop, although it would definitely fit the "tomb-of-the-unknown-vegetable" motif. I began to panic because I knew I could handle a frontal assault by spam alone, but if it ever allied itself with Vienna sausage and liverwurst, I would be dead meat.

Fortunately, I read the parenthetical phrases and realized that spam is a computer term for electronic junk mail. Anytime one believes he is under attack from a questionable meat product, truth seems to take a backseat to exaggeration, uncertainty, and fiction. I wish I had gathered the facts first.

It reminded me of the *Andy Griffith Show* episode where Andy went to the drugstore to get some medication for Barney's nicked trigger finger. Three ladies heard the request, and by the time the story got back to Andy and Barney, Barney had shot himself and died. Don't be too hard on the women. Later, Andy and Barney turned a simple shoe salesman from New York City into a Hollywood talent scout. Gossip knows no gender.

Gossip is only so much spam—verbal junk mail. Although

some may be good at it, gossip was never intended to be a spiritual gift. As Christians we are not only to seek truth, but also to speak it. Will Rogers said it best: "Rumor travels faster, but it don't stay put as long as truth."

Are you tired of being shackled by rumor and gossip? Speak the truth. I have it from a good Source that it will set you free.

IF AN ELEPHANT BAGS A HUNTER, DOES HE TIE HIM TO HIS TRUNK?

It is unsafe to go outdoors if you have horns, sharp teeth, thick fur, webbed feet, no opposable thumbs, or hang by your tail. (However, if you have all of the above, it would greatly improve your chances at the Miss America pageant under their new and somewhat relaxed guidelines.)

One look at all of the grinning husbands with that awkward dear-in-the-headlights look on their face, and we know hunting season has arrived. My dictionary defines *hunt* as "to kill or catch game for food or sport." Wives define *hunt* as "an opportunity for husbands to get away from work for a few days (under the guise of some macho ancestral outdoor shooting ritual) while we are stuck at home to cook meals, work jobs, take the kids to soccer practice at two different locations at the same time, entertain the in-laws who dropped in unexpectedly to offer their opinions, and change a baby diaper that just went through the monsoon season."

Some animals, such as dogs and cats, are illegal to hunt; however, I would be wary of wild game dinners where there is a lot of winking. Other animals are on the endangered species list. They are extremely rare and mostly seen in zoos, on ties, or at endangered species wild-game dinners—with pig sounds and banjo music—in some of the more toothless areas of the rural South.

One of these is the bison, or buffalo. A buffalo is just an alo on a weightlifting program. The buffalo almost became extinct when people got bored really quickly on the plains and tired easily from singing "Oh give me a home . . ." which, at that time, was the only song in the Top 40.

Discouraging words became rampant, so they shot the buffalo. Property values then plummeted because no one wanted a home where the buffalo had roamed. Buffalo were the predecessors to today's teenagers: they ate, had funny hair, and roamed in herds.

My dictionary also defines *hunt* as "to search or seek." It defines *righteous* as "acting in a just, upright manner; doing what is right." Doing what is right could mean being kind to one another, being tenderhearted, and forgiving one another, as in Ephesians 4:32. Have you shown kindness to anyone lately? Have you expressed a tender heart for a friend who is hurting? Have you forgiven someone for a wrong done to you?

When hunters return from a successful hunt, they tie their game to their vehicle's hood or trunk for everyone to see. When

God gets His game, He ties it to a cross and says, "Here, carry this." Carrying a cross is best done without a lot of fanfare or publicity. God is looking for an endangered species, that rare Christian who wants to be like Jesus.

With God hunting season is always open. Are you game?

A Christian Without Joy
Is Like Pomp Without Circumstance

If you blinked last week, you missed the holiday highlight
of the year, and I don't mean Wayne Newton singing "In-
A-Gadda-Da-Vida" to the tune of "Chestnuts Roasting
on an Open Fire" . . . although that would be close. In a Y2K
sort of way, Presidents' Day has come and gone without much
of a whimper.

As a child I celebrated Washington's Birthday by dressing up
in a white wig, tight pants, and funny shoes . . . at least I *hope* it
was for Washington's Birthday. We used to celebrate Lincoln's
Birthday on February 12 and Washington's Birthday on
February 22. Over the years the committee for deciding presidential birthdays decided not only were Lincoln and Washington
born on the same day, but so was every other president. We
celebrate the day, even though no president has ever

been loved by everyone. The closest I ever saw was Blair Clark, president of my sixth-grade class. He was blond, athletic, and intelligent . . . everything a girl wanted in a boy. I had a collection of Mr. Potato Heads.

When we think of presidents, we always think of George Washington, known for crossing the Tupperware River in the dead of winter in a resealable plastic boat, and Abraham Lincoln, who, through a typographical error, treed the slaves. We remember Theodore Roosevelt, who made his army ride sandpaper saddles up San Juan Hill, where they became known as the Rough Riders; Thomas Jefferson, who wrote the Declaration of Independence on the back of his church bulletin during the contemporary worship service; and Gerald Ford, who fell down a lot.

There was also Andrew Johnson, who, along with his brother, Howard, discovered baby shampoo and a chain of hotels. Grover Cleveland was the only president to have a professional football team named after him, although they were never known by their full name, the Grover Cleveland Browns.

William Harrison caught a cold during his rather lengthy inaugural address on March 4, 1841, and died one month later. Doctors now call it Vanna White's disease, Irritable Vowel Syndrome.

At one time these men were famous because of their position—their "Pomp and Circumstance," if you will. I wonder how many of them would associate the presidency with real joy. Society seems to dictate that joy can be found through wealth, power, or success. Eventually, these all fade. Time has a way of bringing memory to its knees.

One of the definitions of *pomp* is "splendor or magnificence." Real joy comes in a continuing relationship with Jesus—pomp, circumstance, and all. Too many Christians have let their circumstances overrule their pomp. We have to choose every day how we will live our lives.

The joyous Christian, because of the magnificence of Christ, can always find pomp in the midst of circumstances.

EXPERIENCING HAPLESS TRIALS
BUT RIDING HAPPY TRAILS

W e have a unique history in America, and there is nothing more unique to us than the number of dead armadillos along our nation's highways. The second
most unique thing about us is the story of the cowboy. The cowboy was invented in Texas in the middle of the nineteenth century
because people in the pioneer areas out West grew weary of eating amber waves of grain and were running out of wild game, with
the exception of *Wheel of Fortune: Beach Party Edition.*

So for food, they looked to Texas, with its wealth of domes-
ticated animals such as pigs, dogs, cats, cows, and Baptist
preachers. Cows were selected because "Pigboys and Indians"
made no sense, there were not enough trees in West Texas for
the dogs, and no one would hear a cat stampede. The last
species was eliminated when no one wanted to spend six

months driving a herd of skinny, unruly Baptist preachers because there were not enough potluck dinners along the trail to keep them fattened.

The cowboys were dirty, dangerous, rowdy, lonely, desperate, and poorly paid. Many of them went on to be youth ministers. Like youth ministers, their main duty was to drive cattle. But since cows have no opposable thumbs, the cowboys were constantly opening car doors during the drive; and the cows, never being content, were always asking, "Are we there yet?" There were a few cows that did not have much to say and just sat around watching their favorite movie, *Dr. Moolittle.*

There were other problems, such as storms, droughts, stampedes, rustlers, a long line at the license renewal center, and an inadequate inventory at the LifeWay Christian Store. At night (after the sky had not been cloudy all day), with the harmonica playing in the background, you can just picture the deer and the antelope playing. You can almost see the cowboys at home on the range sitting around the campfire eating beans . . . which usually led to discouraging words and was the real reason the buffalo roamed.

Although my kids would say I lived during the time of the cowboys, my first exposure to them was in front of the TV set in the late 1950s watching, among others, Roy Rogers, "King of the Cowboys." What I remember about Roy Rogers is that he was always singing and smiling . . . on screen and off. As Christians we have a song to sing, only too many times we seem to have more sour notes than we do smiles.

Sometimes as Christians it seems the whole world knows what we are against but has no idea of what we are for. We somehow manage to point the media to ourselves rather than to God. We must take a stand against sin, but we must also pray for the sinner to find God.

It took a singing cowboy to exemplify to me in a real way the simple words of Jesus: "Be of good cheer; I have overcome the world" (John 16:33 KJV). So long, Roy. Thanks for reminding us that only Jesus can change our sour notes to sweet music and turn our hapless trials into happy trails. *Until we meet again* . . .

DEATH OF A FALSE SALESMAN

Samuel Taylor Coleridge was a nineteenth-century English poet who is credited with this famous rhyme: "Swans sing before they die—'twere no bad thing/ Should certain persons die before they sing." On another note, Edvard Grieg, a Norwegian composer of the nineteenth century, once said these wonderful words: "I am sure my music has the taste of codfish in it."

My music could be compared to Grieg. People have always said my music has the taste of carp. By nature I am a singer. Notice that I said singer and not musician. The sound may be unnatural and shrouded in ambiguity, but the effort is sincere. When my kids or my wife disagree with me, all I have to do to get them back in line is threaten to sing. If my threat includes creative movement, their fear is exceeded only by their terror, and the Chihuahuas clear the room screaming at the top of their little lungs, "Please give the man a chalupa!"

CHAPTER 9: Lessons from the Example of Christ

Along with talking Chihuahuas, there is one other phenomenon associated with my singing. It was 1962, and I was in a church auditorium on a Sunday night with about fifty people in attendance. I had to excuse myself to go to the rest room—complete with tile floor, located directly behind the auditorium.

The back of the auditorium shared a wall with the bathroom. It had all the soundproofing capability of a waffle. As I said by nature I am a singer. Nature called and I began singing. The sound and fury of the sermon paled in comparison to the angelic, melodic voice of a ten-year-old boy reverberating through the waffle wall with "Shall We Gather at the River?"

By the time the suddenly speechless preacher and stunned congregation had recovered from the initial shock and yet innocent timeliness of the words, I was concluding my impromptu concert with a mesmerizing, operatic rendition of the chorus: "Gather with the saints at the river that flows by the throne of God."

Recently I was reminded about a mesmerizing performance by another singer. This particular singer sang a song of doom and destruction several years ago in Waco, Texas. His prophetic lyrics mesmerized hurting people of all ages. However, David Koresh's song ended not on a happy note, but with his death and the deaths of most of his followers. Some of them were children who really didn't want to sing his song.

In Calvin Miller's magnificent narrative *The Singer,* Jesus is the Singer and the gospel is His Song. It is a beautiful metaphor of the incarnation and how the Singer lived and died singing His Song of love and forgiveness. Although we as Christians have a song to sing, we need to be careful about whose song we are singing—for only one song did God write the words.

Chapter 10:

Spending Time with the Holidazed

Lessons from Holidays and Holy Days

GOD HAD A GREAT NOTION—
THE BIRTH OF THE EASTER PEOPLE

I read in a magazine that a man in Southern California was sitting in his hot tub and had a vision of blowing all the smog out of Los Angeles. Or was he sitting in the smog and had a vision of blowing all the hot tubs out of Los Angeles? No, I'm pretty sure it was the first one. (I personally don't care for the image of a man sitting in a hot tub having visions.)

He surmised it could be done with huge gusts of wind. Before I read any further, I pictured him surrounding the city with Academy Award acceptance speeches and guest speakers at banker conventions. His vision actually included placing giant bellows at locations throughout the city. (A bellows is a fireplace tool that you squeeze together to blow air over the coals and get the flame going. In the hands of an amateur, it also blows ashes all over the den, and if placed in the right physiologically sensitive spot can send a surprised Chihuahua airborne.)

His idea is based on the chaos theory of complex systems in mathematics. This theory says that complicated phenomena, such as hospital food, a teenager's mood swings, and how women can carry on three different conversations simultaneously, while men are doing good to make a complete sentence without using the words *golf, football, remote control,* or *bathroom,* are all affected by seemingly unrelated events.

My idea of chaos has always been less complex—a painting and pizza party for thirty-five unattended preschoolers inside a china shop with no bathrooms. The chaos theory says there are certain days when all the right meteorological and liturgical factors are in place, thus enabling a large bellows to create a wind current strong enough to sweep the smog out to sea. Of course to create enough wind current to get rid of all the smog in Los Angeles, it would take three hundred bellows, one national political convention, three men sharing a golf story, or twenty Baptist preachers.

Where do these ridiculous ideas come from? I haven't heard of such a far-fetched notion since God devised a plan to save the world from its sin by sending His only Son, Jesus, to die on a cross. Can you imagine? The people in Jerusalem certainly did not buy into it. Some of His closest followers failed to believe it. It was a chaotic time. But out of the chaos of the Cross comes the relativity of the Resurrection.

God's notion to give us a second chance is the story of Easter . . . rebirth . . . a notion conceived in heaven. God takes the spiritual smog in our lives and blows it away, not with a bellows but through the sweet breath of His Holy Spirit. His notion was for us to be "born again," but because we often slip into our former attitudes and habits, we discover part of the lifelong process of being born again . . . having to continually cut the unbiblical cord.

DUTY, HONOR, AND ABOVE ALL . . . A REALLY GOOD SALES PITCH

I
t is April 1995. America celebrates the fiftieth anniversary of the United States' victory in the last great battle
of World War II, the invasion of Okinawa, an island 350
miles off the coast of Japan. By the time the battle had ended,
180,000 U.S. combat troops had been involved, and the total
number of casualties reached 50,000 killed or wounded, the
most of any battle during the Pacific War.

Over the years veterans have returned to places like
Okinawa, Iwo Jima, Guadalcanal, Normandy, Anzio, and others, to visit the battlefields. They pay their respects to fallen
comrades. They think about the impact of what they did. They
shed a tear. They remember.

It is November 1995. It is the thirtieth anniversary of the
United States' "victory" in the first major battle of the Vietnam
War, the Battle of the Ia Drang Valley, a valley in west-central

CHAPTER 10: Lessons from Holidays and Holy Days

South Vietnam near the Cambodian border. This battle was brought to our attention once again in a movie with Mel Gibson based on Colonel Hal Moore's book, *We Were Soldiers Once . . . and Young.* It was also chronicled in the book *In Retrospect*, by Robert McNamara.

Colonel Moore was the commanding officer of the Ia Drang forces. American losses totaled three hundred men. It was a battle that told the American high command that this would be a very long war and not easily won—hence, my quotation marks around the word "victory."

Veterans have seldom returned to visit the battlefields of the Ia Drang Valley, Khe Sanh, Pleiku, Dak To, and Happy Valley in Vietnam. They have seldom returned to the Chosin Reservoir, Pork Chop Hill, Inchon, and Pusan in Korea. In their own way, they pay their respects to fallen comrades. They think about the impact of what they did. They shed a tear. They remember.

It is May 2004. It is Memorial Day, and people everywhere are talking about how they will spend the weekend. For many the festivities will include eating grilled burgers and drinking beer. They will have trouble remembering anything.

Somewhere between the history books, the sales spectaculars at the mall, and the beer fest at the lake, we have lost the real meaning of this important holiday. It seems the further away we get from these events, the less we remember.

For the sake of those who fought and died, we *must* remember. They were different wars with different battle plans and strategies. There were different reactions on the home front. There was a common thread. Men fought and died . . . and millions of lives were affected forever.

Yes, we must remember, for it is in our remembering that we say thank you. In that moment maybe one more veteran, no matter which war, will realize his service was not in vain. Maybe we all will understand that freedom would not be possible were it not for their sacrifices. On this day, remembering is our personal memorial to those who did not return.

IN SEARCH OF THANKSGIVING

To fully understand the first Thanksgiving in 1621 and its future impact on turkeys, we must go back to 1609 and a French explorer named Samuel de Champlain. Champlain founded Quebec, discovered the St. Lawrence River, and almost had an expensive bubbly beverage named after him (not to be confused with the German explorer, Samuel de Budweiser, who discovered St. Louis).

Champlain wanted to make war against the Iroquois Indians, the most feared tribe in the American wilderness, except for the Washington Redskins, feared most for their ticket scalping. He formed a bond with several tribes referred to as the Five Nations: *Cayuga* (which sounds very much like an old car horn), *Onondaga* (named after an Indian Foot Race called the Onondaga 500), *Mohawk* (which in English means "more predatory bird"), *Oneida* (feared because of their fine throwing knives), and *Tupperware* (the least-feared Indians around because they used plastic arrows).

The difference between Champlain and the Pilgrims, who followed later, was that Champlain tried to befriend the Indians. The Pilgrims, being typical Americans, tried to use the Indians for what they could get out of them. Some of the Indians did not appreciate this new capitalist approach and became extremely hostile—killing, torturing, eating, or enslaving their enemies. Their descendants did really well in law school.

One of them, Samoset, was the first Indian to graduate from the electoral college. He eventually ran for public office in Jamestown, amid some controversy, against a local Spaniard named Manual Recounts. The local newscast projected Samoset the winner two days before both precincts closed. There was a lot of confusion, and the ballots were sent to Florida.

Samoset became frustrated, got gored by an animal, and went back to the bush. Manual Recounts won. Before Samoset left the Pilgrims, he introduced them to the Wampanogs, who showed them how to plant crops. These were not the same Indians as the Wampaneggnogs, who showed them how to drink a lot.

When the first harvest came in that fall, the Pilgrims were very thankful. Before that first Thanksgiving, life had been rough, and food was at a premium. We have celebrated ever since with different family traditions on Thanksgiving.

When I was in high school, we played our biggest rival on Thanksgiving morning at 10:00, the last game of the season. We had no high-school playoff system in those years. We still had time to eat a hearty afternoon feast of turkey, dressing, rolls, the horribly misnamed giblet gravy, and some green things.

I have discovered something about thanksgiving. It is more than a meal. It is more than a holiday. It is not always a proper noun. Thanksgiving, for the Christian, is a verb. It is something we do.

It is always appropriate to give thanks to God, but when was the last time you gave thanks to people for what they have meant to you? Find some friends and tell them, and don't wait until next November to do it again. Discover the beauty of thanksgiving.

Even if we haven't been thanksgiven, we have an obligation to be thanksgiving.

INTERESTING CONCEPT—
BEING STONED ON VALENTINE'S DAY

When I was in the sixth grade, I was king of my class. I had power then that I have not felt since. There was a brief period of time when I thought I would have power again. I got over it when my children became teenagers.

In sixth grade I could smile while walking through the cafeteria at lunch, and all the fifth- and sixth-grade girls would ooh and ahh, scream with delight, and swoon back and forth. It was not until later that I was told they were mostly screaming and swooning from nausea, because I had a chunk of chewed food the size of a walnut between my teeth.

Actually, I was very shy around girls. Let's just say that my idea of flirting with a girl was to put a tack in her chair. It was unique, short, and to the point. However, as I got older,

I realized that girls didn't appreciate that kind of direct approach.

The best part of sixth grade was Valentine's Day. I looked forward to it because I could send valentines to girls just for the heck of it, and not because I had to . . . like in a marriage. I always picked out a special valentine with a special message for that one special girl, so she could read it and then toss it into a special wastebasket. It was a special moment.

Valentine's Day made me wary of females and scarred me for life. Nonetheless, I passed out valentines with gusto . . . Alfredo Gusto, an exchange student from Italy. Not only did I give valentines, but I received them, and that was even better because I got valentines from girls who I didn't think knew I existed . . . except when they sat in their chair. I was pretty tacky.

I especially liked receiving the little candy hearts with engraved jewels of romantic wisdom like "Be My Valentine," "Call Me," "You Are Nice," and "You Have a Huge Piece of Chewed Food between Your Teeth." The big one I always anticipated said, "I Love You."

Someone else was in the valentine business long before Valentine's Day became a reality. God began the process when He created the world, continued it when He gave Eve to Adam, and has been doing it ever since.

The Bible is full of expressions of God's love for mankind. My favorite concerns the woman caught in adultery. On the brink of her being stoned, Jesus stepped in and said that whoever was without sin could throw first.

Hmm . . . some things never change. Even today, Christians

always seem poised to throw a stone. In Jesus Christ, God has sent the world the ultimate valentine. All a person has to do is open it. Have you looked around lately? A lot of valentines remain unopened.

I wonder if part of the reason is that we as Christians have become so proficient at throwing stones we have forgotten how to send valentines. It is difficult to help someone open an envelope when your hands are full of rocks.

THE HIGH COST OF LIVING
IN THE LAND OF THE FREE

F lies everywhere are sharpening their fangs and getting
their little quadnoculars in focus, because we are entering
one of the busiest, and most who-cares-about-cholesterol-
and-sunburn weekends of the year—the celebration of
Memorial Day. There will be more people at the lake, more
people in golf course woods retrieving errant shots (with me, a
good Baptist, I do herewith solemnly believe that my shots are
inerrant), and more people cooking outdoors than almost any
other weekend.

And why not! This is that special fast-food-restaurant-
theme-toy-lacking holiday we hearty, burger-loving Americans
celebrate every year. We do this to honor those poor unsuspecting souls who, armed with only their pocketbook, have died
during heavy traffic while invading the shopping malls and
doing their part to make our Norman Rockwellesque country

safe for credit cards. At least it would seem so to someone recently arriving from another planet . . . or Los Angeles.

In reality, Memorial Day is supposed to be a time when we remember who we are as a country and honor those who died in the process of writing that definition in blood. No matter the size of the war, death always is able to establish a foothold—particularly in places like the Ardennes in France, Anzio in Italy, the Chosin Reservoir in Korea, and the swamps of the Mekong Delta in South Vietnam.

In order to fully understand what it means to be an American, we must never forget Bastogne in Belgium, Pusan in South Korea, the A Shau Valley (Hamburger Hill) in Vietnam, and a thousand more like them—because each one of those names represents a place, and in each of those places, America has left a piece of her soul.

What about the thousands of aircraft shot down and hundreds of ships sunk in places that will forever be nameless in the minds of today's generation? Have you heard of the Sullivans from World War II? Five brothers joined the navy and were assigned to the same ship, the cruiser *Juneau*. The *Juneau* was sunk by the Japanese in November 1942, during the battle of the Solomon Islands. Four brothers went down with the ship; the fifth died in a life raft.

That is why we have Memorial Day—to remember. We remember because it is a vital part of our inheritance and because the survivors need to see that the sacrifice of their fallen brothers and sisters was not in vain. This is always a most difficult time for the survivors.

This weekend, as you fire up the grill, be prepared for your mind to wander. When it does, let it focus on the figure of a small boy standing at his father's military funeral, saluting with one hand and holding a flag in the other, while off in the distance a solitary bugle is sounding "Taps." Allow yourself to shed a tear . . . and in that one shining moment, you will have experienced Memorial Day.

WEARY FROM MAKING MOUNTAINS OUT OF MOLEHILLS? TRY REVERSING THE PROCESS

n my younger days as a youth minister, I was undaunted. In fact, when I was at seminary, I had the foresight to have my daunt surgically removed. Nowhere was this more evident than on my first youth ski trip. (Now that I am fifty and a minister of education, my daunt is back. In fact, the most risky thing I do now is drink regular coffee after eight at night.)

Back to my first ski trip. It was Winter Park, Colorado, in April 1986. It was me and my athletic ability against the mountain. The mountain won. Hands down. Hands up. Hands in the trees. Hands with a death-defying grip on the ski poles. Hands everywhere.

Other formerly attached body parts were scattered over the bunny slopes. I landed in the most heinously contorted body configurations known to mankind, positions once thought possible only through a macabre game of Stephen King–led "Twister." I was not a pretty sight.

My road to incompetence was paved with well-intentioned and well-paid-for ski lessons. After the first fifteen minutes of the first lesson, my classmates (all under the age of twelve) concluded that I was a toad. Over the next three hours, I did nothing to alter their amazingly astute observation.

Because I never mastered the somewhat timely art of changing direction (not to mention the somewhat timelier art of actually stopping), the plastic temporary fences around me had an unusually short life span. I fared no better once we took the chairlift to the top.

Draped with enough ski equipment to hunt wolverines, I was unprepared for the concept of jumping out of a moving chair and remaining upright. In my efforts to wedge, turn, or stop, I wiped out fourteen people, three fences, seven bushes, and one completely surprised moose. For the safety of everyone, I quit. I had no intention of walking in those designed-by-Frankenstein boots that did not inspire Nancy Sinatra's "These Boots Were Made for Walkin'," so I called a toad truck and got a lift.

In the twilight of my ski years, I have found the words to an old adage to be quite comforting: When the going gets tough, the really inept skiers go to the lodge and drink hot chocolate.

On that ski trip, the mountain won. On the night of the Crucifixion, the disciples faced their own "mountain." Jesus was dead. All hope was gone, or so it appeared. God had other plans. Enter the Resurrection. In a new twist on an old saying, the mountain became a molehill.

The season of Lent serves as preparation for Easter. Easter

is hope in the midst of hopelessness, love in the depths of hatred, and encouragement at the height of depression. Through faith in God's power—illustrated uniquely in the Resurrection—any mountain can become a molehill. For you see, God does not necessarily change the mountain. He does change our perspective. See you on the slopes.

TAKING GOD'S NAME IN VAIN
IS NOT ALWAYS DONE WITH WORDS

August 1999—A research firm in California is granted $10 million to study the idea of forgiveness. Psychologists, sociologists, and neuroscientists form the nucleus of the Campaign for Forgiveness Research. The name of God or Jesus is never mentioned.

August 1993—The pope makes a rare visit to the United States and speaks to seventy-five thousand people at Mile High Stadium in Denver, Colorado. However, the main news story out of Denver is not the pope's views on several key issues but what the street vendors have for sale. Pope hats, caps, pens, and T-shirts are all the rage. The best/worst is the coffee mug. When it is filled with hot liquid, through some form of chemical reaction, an image of the pope appears on the outside of the mug. I'll have one confession espresso to go.

March 1993—Hundreds of thousands of people brave the

hot sun in Agoo, Philippines, waiting for an appearance by the Virgin Mary. The crowd is there because a twelve-year-old child claims to have seen her on the first Saturday of every month since 1989. Vendors have a brisk business hawking T-shirts, food, water, and various Jesus-related souvenirs. Making a profit on the Prophet is not limited to television.

September 1992—Several thousand people in Marlboro Township, New Jersey, stand in heavy rain hoping to see the Virgin Mary. They are there because one of the local towns-people claims that since 1988 Mary has appeared in his back-yard on the first Sunday of every month. The cost of getting a glimpse of Mary? The view is free, but parking is $5.00.

October 1985—A picture (with explanation) appears in a Little Rock, Arkansas, newspaper showing the founder of a small religious toy company marketing her new Baby Jesus Doll. The newspaper quoted her as saying, "I think that people are getting to the point where they want something to believe in again, and I believe anyone who is a Christian would want one." The thirteen-inch vinyl doll comes with a manger, a non-toxic glow-in-the-dark detachable halo, and a card with the words: "My name is Jesus. Jesus loves you. I am your friend. Please love me." The price of Jesus's love? The love is free, but the doll is $31.50.

April c. 33 AD—A few people are gathered below three crosses on a lonely hill outside Jerusalem. They are there to watch a man die. At the foot of the middle cross, Roman sol-diers are casting lots for the bloodstained garments of a man called Jesus. They, too, are collecting souvenirs.

When the soldiers left Jesus that day, their hands were full. Is that how we are to leave the Cross? As Christians we are to minister to others, but we cannot reach out to a hurting neighbor with our arms filled with souvenirs, in whatever form that might be. We cannot hold on to old habits or poor attitudes. We cannot hold on to anything that would keep us from grabbing hold of Jesus.

What are we holding on to? If we have truly met Jesus at the Cross, our hands will be empty . . . but our hearts will be full.

WE THREE KINGS OF ORIENT 'R' US

We interrupt the regularly scheduled shopping frenzy to bring you this special news bulletin: *There are only fifteen days until Christmas.* That means fifteen days to buy socks, underwear, lawn implement tools, or discounted cologne gift packs for that certain someone.

Have you ever noticed after about fifteen years of marriage that romance and sentimentality give way to economics and practicality? Jewelry and appliances are replaced with salad spoons and grip-lock pliers. It happens because men and shopping go together like female wrestlers and charm school.

At any mall during the holiday season, herds of men can be observed wandering aimlessly beside their wives. The men who do not survive the walk hunker down forlornly on the husband benches. Innocent children pass by with parents, and the conversation goes something like this: "Mommy, why are those men sitting there with their mouths open and their eyes glazed over? Are they in a coma or have they been watching too much football?" Parent responds: "No, Son; their wives are shopping."

There are several complicated procedures involved in male-pattern shopping. The first step is to choose between going shopping or giving ourselves an appendectomy. If we want to keep our honeys happy, we choose shopping.

The next step is to plan the approach. Do we shop together or do we separate? Here is an important tip for novice shopping husbands. Once inside the mall, proceed to the nearest women's clothing store. When you arrive, point to the first outfit you see and say, "Honey, I love that. Get it and let's go look at power tools." The more the outfit resembles a window covering, the quicker she will say, "Why don't we separate?"

With mission accomplished and a smirk on your face, you may head for the power tools, big-screen TVs, and cheese logs. Be sure and stop at the toy store to find this year's hot toy doll, Belch-and-Spit Bubba, predicted to be big in Alabama.

I love giving and receiving presents. I do a pretty good job of giving "things" at Christmas, but I am always reminded of the poor job I do in giving of myself throughout the year. I could do better in giving my family and friends more time, love, patience, kindness, encouragement, and a lot of other gifts that do not require standing in line.

This season also makes us think about what gifts we bring to Jesus. It is so easy to be kind, giving, and encouraging at Christmas. We, like the three kings, bear these gifts with much sincerity during the holiday season. But unlike the gifts of the kings, these gifts are not to be left at the manger; they are to be taken with us—used over and over again.

At this time of year, "We Three Kings of Orient Are" is a wonderful hymn about giving gifts to the King. An even better one is "Give of Your Best to the Master."

IF YOU STAND AT THE MANGER, YOU CAN SEE THE CROSS

His name was Zorthon. Just by looking at him I knew he was from another planet, in another galaxy, in another star system . . . or San Francisco. Until that moment my only contact with alien life forms had been watching college football players eat lunch.

His people understood the meaning of every holiday celebration except for Easter and Christmas. His mission was to discover the true meaning of Christmas.

His instructions first led him to contact a "Santa Claus" at the North Pole, but by the time he arrived, Santa was gone and the trail was cold. He hurried to his ship, turned on his radar, and set a course for the big blip on the screen that was shaking like a bowl full of jelly.

Catching up to Santa in Iceland, Zorthon had a nice visit

with Prancer and Rudolph. They told him that Santa's part was only to take toys to boys and girls all over the free world and Texas. Dasher overheard the conversation. He suggested Zorthon go to the city and watch people in their natural habitat as they observed the hanging of the greed.

Once in the city, Zorthon stopped in a seedy part of town and found some men in various stages of disarray, lying in gutters and secluded doorways. They assumed Zorthon was one of them and talked freely with him.

He asked them about Christmas, but all they could tell him was that it came once a year and usually passed them by. They thought they saw Christmas once, but it was only a reflection in an ice patch of a cross on top of the church steeple.

Leaving discouraged, Zorthon made a couple of stops at what he understood to be office Christmas parties, hoping to find at least a clue, but everyone was clueless. He didn't hear or see anything intelligible, so he left more frustrated than ever.

As a last-ditch effort, he decided to visit the most dangerous place his leaders had warned him about: a shopping mall. When he entered the mall, he realized in a nanosecond that it was even more terrifying than watching people eat slugs on *Fear Factor*. The people were so busy being rude and insensitive he had no chance to talk to anyone about Christmas.

In utter dismay he made his way back to his ship and called Zod. He informed Zod that as an outsider looking in, he could not possibly comprehend what Christmas was all about. The only way he could ever see Christmas would be to stay here and become an earthling himself.

Unknowingly, Zorthon reached the first step in understanding Christmas. God has come to earth in the form of a baby, and through that baby He is offering the world the gift of life. If we really want to see Christmas, we must understand that the manger ultimately leads to the cross.

FOR UNTO YOU A SAVIOR IS BORN—
DO NOT DELETE

Having recently entered the world of the Internet and e-mail, I am a little fuzzy on the terminology used in sending messages. I am uncomfortable telling someone I am surfing the Web. I feel like I ought to be listening to the Beach Boys, and I will never become a Web browser because it sounds like a spider looking for companionship.

My computer tells me I could have "hostile Java." I hate flavored coffees, especially angry ones. The closest I ever came to a cup of hostile coffee was in a truck stop poured by a much-too-chummy waitress named Al.

My manual also tells me I could have "cookies" in my computer that might have to be deleted. I prefer leted cookies, but it doesn't scare me. As a child I survived Ginger Snaps in Vacation Bible School, or was she on *Gilligan's Island*? I discovered most of my problems would go away if I delete my ID. Freud would be proud.

I was also warned I could have an "active desktop." I haven't had an active desktop since third grade. On another screen I was introduced to "bugs" and "viruses." It went like this: "Mr. Babb, meet Mr. Virus. Mr. Bugs, meet Mr. Babb." Viruses are bad, but they can be attacked by something called "quick backup," which could also be the result of a bad meat loaf.

The best news is my computer has "smell check." I have always had a problem with smelling. My children also have a problem with smelling. They get it from their father. I have told them not to worry about how horribly they smell, just look nice while they are smelling.

My teachers always told me they had never had a student who smelled as bad as I did. They gave me extra work, and it made me feel good on that rare occasion when they were proud of the way I smelled. With smell check, it is reassuring to know my problems with smelling can be corrected by simply clicking my moose.

Like a good computer geek, I check my e-mail every day. Most of the time it says, "Hi, Martin.Babb! You have no messages." It is definitely a downer in starting the day. It makes me think about the people who probably not only begin their day, but end it with no messages. What a shame, especially at Christmas, because the essence of Christmas is the fact that they *do* have a message!

For unto you a Savior is born! God has downloaded His Son in order to delete our sin and in the process upgrade our lives. Unlike e-mail messages, God's message at Christmas is sent to everyone. We can accept it and do nothing, or we can forward it to someone else. Do it now, and see the world through the eyes of the Christmas manger . . . the ultimate rom with a view.